WEBER AND DURKHEIM

Weber and Durkheim: A methodological comparison is a systematic, comparative analysis of the methodologies of Max Weber and Émile Durkheim. Jensen shows how Weber and Durkheim analyse Protestants and Catholics in practice in *The Protestant Ethic* and *Suicide*, respectively. The very different ways that Weber and Durkheim carry out their analyses are then used to describe, analyse and contrast their methodological principles and points of view, raising fundamental questions in sociological and social science analysis, such as:

- What constitutes the object of sociology?
- How are concepts developed?
- What status can be attributed to laws?
- Which possibilities – and limitations – do we have for producing scientific insight into society?
- What are we to think of the relationship between 'Is' and 'Ought' – and how can social science deal with values?
- How are social phenomena to be explained?

This book will be a valuable resource for students and scholars of sociology, social methodology, political theory, political science, social theory and philosophy.

Henrik Jensen, Dr.Scient.Pol. and Ph.D. in Political Science, is a Professor in the Department of Political Science at the University of Copenhagen and has written and lectured on social science methodology.

WEBER AND DURKHEIM

A methodological comparison

Henrik Jensen

LONDON AND NEW YORK

First published 2012
by Routledge
2 Park Square, Milton Park, Abingdon, Oxon OX14 4RN

Simultaneously published in the USA and Canada
by Routledge
711 Third Avenue, New York, NY 10017

Routledge is an imprint of the Taylor & Francis Group,
an informa business

© 2012 Henrik Jensen

The right of Henrik Jensen to be identified as author of this
work has been asserted by him in accordance with the
Copyright, Designs and Patents Act 1988.

All rights reserved. No part of this book may be reprinted
or reproduced or utilized in any form or by any electronic,
mechanical, or other means, now known or hereafter
invented, including photocopying and recording, or in any
information storage or retrieval system, without permission
in writing from the publishers.

British Library Cataloguing in Publication Data
A catalogue record for this book is available from the
British Library

Library of Congress Cataloging in Publication Data
Jensen, Henrik, 1947–
  Weber and Durkheim: a methodological
comparison/Henrik Jensen. – 1st ed.
  p. cm.
  Includes bibliographical references.
  1. Social sciences–Methodology. 2. Weber, Max,
1864–1920–Political and social views. 3. Durkheim,
Émile, 1858–1917–Political and social views. I. Title.
  H61.J46 2012
  300.1–dc23
  2011049079

ISBN: 978–0–415–69614–2 (hbk)
ISBN: 978–0–415–69615–9 (pbk)
ISBN: 978–0–203–11585–5 (ebk)

Typeset in Bembo and Stone Sans by
Florence Production Ltd, Stoodleigh, Devon

To Egil

CONTENTS

Acknowledgements	ix
Abbreviations	xi

1 Weber and Durkheim — 1

Weber and Durkheim: a methodological comparison 1
Why Weber and Durkheim? 2
Methodology and research practice in Weber and
* Durkheim 3*
'How' Weber and Durkheim? 5

2 Analysing Protestants and Catholics — 9

Durkheim: Protestants, Catholics – and suicide 9
Weber: Protestants, Catholics – and capitalism 16

3 'Social ontology' — 23

Weber: a chaos perception 23
Durkheim: a cosmos perception 26

4 Epistemology — 30

Durkheim: inductivism 30
Weber: neo-Kantianism 34

viii Contents

5   Science and values   38
Weber: the gulf between 'Is' and 'Ought' 38
Durkheim: the bridge between 'Is' and 'Ought' 43

6   Methodological individualism   48
Weber: methodological individualism 49
Durkheim: methodological collectivism 52

7   Types of explanation   56
Durkheim: functional and causal explanations 56
Weber: intentional and causal explanations 60

8   Formation of concepts   69
Weber: ideal types 69
Durkheim: generic concepts 73

9   Laws   76
Durkheim: laws as an end 76
Weber: laws as means 79

10   Weber and Durkheim: a methodological
       comparison   84
Weber and Durkheim: two methodologies, two
  sociologies? 84
Methodological principles and research practice in
  Weber and Durkheim 86

Notes   90
Bibliography   118

ACKNOWLEDGEMENTS

This book has fulfilled its purpose if it helps students and others with an interest in Weber and Durkheim and methodology to obtain an understanding of Weber's and Durkheim's respective methodologies and approaches to sociology and the social sciences.

The book is a lightly revised translation of a Danish book from 2005 (*Weber og Durkheim – en metodologisk sammenligning*, Copenhagen Political Studies Press). I would like once again to express my gratitude for comments on the content of the Danish version of the book from now-retired Professor at CBS, Egil Fivelsdal and Honorary Professor of Sociology, University of Copenhagen, Hans Henrik Bruun. I would also like to thank Noel Parker and Terry Mayer for their comments on the English manuscript, and Rosie Stewart for turning the manuscript into a book. I am further indebted to Lorna Wildgaard, The Royal Danish Library, and Jennifer Dodd, Routledge, for their great assistance in procuring the required permissions to use the quotations. Further, I owe my gratitude to Hans Henrik Bruun, who, along with Professor Sam Whimster, editor of *Max Weber Studies*, has been very helpful in providing the quotations from Weber in English from their forthcoming version of Weber's *GAW*. I thank publishers Routledge, Mohr Siebäck, Presses Universitaires de France and Simon & Schuster

x Acknowledgements

for their help with the permissions to use the quotations. All of the quotations in English from Weber and Durkheim are reproduced in parallel in German and French in the notes. All of the italics in the English quotes are my own. Only square parentheses with initials HJ, [HJ], in English, German or French quotations are mine. However, as my native language is not English, German or French, I wish, last but not least, to thank Jon Jay Neufeld for his great and invaluable help in translating the book. Any inadequacies in the text are most likely my responsibility. The book is dedicated to Egil Fivelsdal, who has done much in Scandinavia in order to stimulate the interest in classics such as Weber and Durkheim.

Henrik Jensen
Copenhagen, 2011

ABBREVIATIONS

The Rules: Émile Durkheim, 1950 (1938): *The Rules of Sociological Method* (translated by Sarah A. Solovay and John H. Mueller and edited by George E.G. Catlin), Glencoe, Illinois: The Free Press.

Suicide: Émile Durkheim, 2010 (1952): *Suicide: A Study in Sociology* (translated by John A. Spaulding and George Simpson and edited, with an introduction, by George Simpson), London and New York: Routledge.

CMW: Max Weber, 2011: *Collected Methodological Writings* (edited by Hans Henrik Bruun and Sam Whimster, translated by Hans Henrik Bruun), London and New York: Routledge.

BSC: Max Weber, 2009 (2004): 'Basic Sociological Concepts' (translated by Keith Tribe), in Sam Whimster (ed.): *The Essential Weber: A Reader*, London and New York: Routledge, pp. 311–58.

The Protestant Ethic: Max Weber, 2010: *The Protestant Ethic and the Spirit of Capitalism* (translated by Talcott Parsons, with an introduction by Anthony Giddens), London and New York: Routledge.

LRLMS: Émile Durkheim, 1981 (1895): *Les règles de la méthode sociologique*, Paris: Quadrige/PUF.

xii Abbreviations

LS: Émile Durkheim, 1981 (1897): *Le suicide – étude de sociologie*, Paris: Quadrige/PUF.

GAW:[1] Max Weber, 1982 (1922): *Gesammelte Aufsätze zur Wissenschafts-lehre* (fünfte erneut durchgesehene Auflage herausgegeben von Johannes Winckelmann), Tübingen: Verlag von J.C.B. Mohr (Paul Siebeck).

DPE: Max Weber 1981 (1904–5): *Die protestantische Ethik I. Eine Aufsatzsammlung* (herausgegeben von Johannes Winckelmann), Gütersloh: Gütersloher Verlagshaus Mohn.

1

WEBER AND DURKHEIM

Weber and Durkheim: a methodological comparison

This book is a systematic, comparative analysis of the methodologies of Max Weber and Émile Durkheim. In this context, the term 'methodologies' does not refer to techniques for the collection and analysis of qualitative or quantitative data. Instead, it refers to Weber's and Durkheim's views on the fundamental principles for how sociological and social science analysis is to be carried out optimally so as to produce valid knowledge.

The comparison focuses on a number of select, but fundamental, questions in sociological and social science analysis: What constitutes the object of sociology? How are concepts developed? What characterizes satisfactory explanations? What status can be attributed to laws? Which possibilities – and limitations – do we have for producing scientific insight into society? What are we to think of the relationship between 'Is' and 'Ought' – and how can social science deal with values?

Against this background, it should be clear that it is not Weber's and Durkheim's research results as sociologists that render them interesting in this context. Nevertheless, it is worth mentioning that

2 Weber and Durkheim

Weber did not unconditionally accept the sociologist label, and that his enormous intellectual capacity and research activity extended to academic fields beyond sociology. For much of his university career, Weber's affiliation was as an honorary professor, and he is difficult to categorize academically. Weber (1864–1920), who studied law, history and philosophy, delivered a lecture on research late in his career in which he referred to himself as an 'economist' (*GAW*: 582, 593). In the same connection, he himself indicated that sociology, history, economics and political science were among the subjects he found most interesting (*GAW*: 600). In 1909, Weber was involved in the creation of a German sociological association, but it was not until later in his authorship that he first used the term sociology in relation to himself.

Conversely, Durkheim (1858–1917), educated at the French elite institution *École Normale Superieure* and with a background in philosophy, was employed within the university framework for most of his academic career and worked in research and teaching. As opposed to Weber, Durkheim identified himself as a sociologist early on and worked towards gaining recognition for sociology as an independent scientific discipline.[1]

Weber and Durkheim have in common that they are not methodologists in the sense that they wrote exclusively about, and only interested themselves in, methodological questions. On the contrary, both of them invested more of their time in carrying out empirical analyses. As such, both of them are interested in method and methodological questions as scientific means as opposed to ends in themselves. This gives good reason to deal with Weber and Durkheim. As already mentioned, however, it is not their sociological results, but instead how such results are produced, that is the object of analysis in the present work.

Why Weber and Durkheim?

If Karl Marx is regarded as a 'Marxist' as opposed to a sociologist, Weber and Durkheim – presumably in that order – are conventionally considered the two greatest figures in modern sociology,[2] and interest in Weber and Durkheim as the 'founding fathers' of sociology has by no means withered, just as their 'classic' status has in no way weakened

– quite the contrary.[3] The robust, 'classic' status of these two scholars in itself therefore justifies the value of examining their thoughts. Moreover, their views on methodology are strikingly different on a number of important points.[4] Furthermore, even though Weber and Durkheim were contemporaries and presumably aware of each other's existence, they never engaged in open dialogue with one another about fundamental methodological questions.

This relationship has inspired speculation to the extent that some have talked about the 'Weber–Durkheim unawareness puzzle' and speculated as to the extent to which they were familiar with one another and, if they were, through which channels. This has even resulted in a fictive 'reconstruction' of the dialogue that they – possibly – could have engaged in with one another, had they actually been in open debate. None of these leads in the 'Weber–Durkheim unawareness puzzle' is to be pursued here,[5] although that renders a systematic confrontation of Weber and Durkheim no less called for.

There is another significant reason to display interest in their respective methodological views. Both Weber and Durkheim were able to overcome the intellectual and scientific division of labour, which has continued to develop since the two laid down their pens. Both scholars not only reflected on how social science investigation and analysis are to be carried out, they both also 'got their hands dirty' with empirical data and carried out concrete studies and analyses based on general assumptions and hypotheses. In that sense, they are quite familiar with the problems of carrying out empirical analyses. When studying Weber and Durkheim, there is therefore less risk of the methodological considerations remaining abstract and noncommittal instructions as to how concrete analyses are to be carried out. In other words, the danger of seeing methodological reflections degenerate into little more than anaemic philosophical discussions, detached from any concrete research practice, is correspondingly lessened.

Methodology and research practice in Weber and Durkheim

The fact that Weber and Durkheim both carried out research and advanced independent methodological considerations contributes

4 Weber and Durkheim

to expectations about a relatively close connection between their methodological views and their research practices, or how they approach a concrete scientific study.

The expectations regarding such a close relationship between methodology and research practice appear to be most justified in the case of Durkheim. This is primarily because Durkheim published a single work devoted to method, *The Rules of the Sociological Method* (*Les règles de la méthode sociologique*), which must be regarded as the most important source of his views on method. The title leaves the reader with the impression that Durkheim probably did not feel as though he had merely written *some* rules for sociological method, but rather that he had arrived at *the* rules for *the* sociological method. Thus, the book presents explicit instructions or maxims for how sociologists ought to approach the research process, for example in connection with observation, classification, explanation, etc. And, in keeping with his ambitions for the field of sociology, Durkheim more than suggests that methodological instructions ought to be included as part of a separate education in sociology. Moreover, there is a brief temporal connection between *The Rules*, which was published in book form in 1895, and Durkheim's two great works, *The Division of Labour in Society* (*De la division du travail social*) and *Suicide* (*Le suicide – étude de sociologie*), which were published in 1893 and 1897, respectively.[6]

The situation is somewhat different with respect to Weber. As opposed to Marx, Weber's methodological reflections are anything but rudimentary. Nonetheless, Weber never produced any such comprehensive *Wissenschaftslehre* – a single work devoted to method. Instead, his views on methodology are found in various articles and essays written at different times, on different issues, in different contexts and, in some cases, probably without ever being fully completed. Against that background, it might seem somewhat disingenuous that, after his death, Weber's widow, Marianne Weber, apparently compiled his most important methodological contributions in a book entitled *Gesammelte Aufsätze zur Wissenschaftslehre* (*GAW*), or *Collected Methodological Writings* (*CMW*).[7] The problem relating to the fact that Weber himself did not compile the *Wissenschaftslehre* as a book is only exacerbated by the fact that Weber's works in *CMW/GAW* cover almost a twenty-year period of time, stretching from around 1903 until his death in 1920. It is therefore hardly surprising – perhaps only human – if Weber's views shifted slightly in the period covered. In his later methodological writings in *CMW/GAW*, that is, from around 1913, Weber thus accepts and operates with the term 'sociology' and refers to his own conception of sociology as 'interpretive sociology' (*verstehende Soziologie*). Moreover, Weber is definitely neither as explicit nor as ambitious as Durkheim in terms of formulating methodological instructions. Durkheim is thus unafraid of advancing methodological instructions for action in italics as 'rules for observations', 'rules for explanation', 'rules for classification', etc. These rules tell sociologists what they ought to do and, in some instances, also what they should avoid doing. Depending on how they are accounted for, Durkheim advances at least ten such rules for prospective sociologists to follow. Weber does not make the same effort towards producing more or less ready-for-use instructions for how colleagues and future students in the field ought to go about analysis in the social sciences or sociology. And finally, Weber's writing style is more complicated than Durkheim's. At the same time, parts of Weber's contributions – and, for that matter, some of Durkheim's writings as well – may be written in concealed polemic dialogue with others.

The factors referred to all appear to pose obstacles for a comparison of the respective methodologies developed by Weber and Durkheim.[8] Against that background, it is worth briefly accounting for the approach pursued in the present work.

'How' Weber and Durkheim?

The approach I have chosen is best illustrated using Table 1.1 and can be characterized as minimalistic, perhaps even 'naive'. Both the table and the approach it reflects have deliberately been kept simple, for the table builds on a number of concrete delimitations.

The following analysis is primarily concentrated on comparing Weber's and Durkheim's methodologies by examining how they believe sociology and social science analysis are to be carried out. Figuratively speaking, this corresponds to most of the analysis occupying the highest horizontal level in Table 1.1. In doing this, the focus is more on 'what they say one is to do' and less on 'what they actually

6 Weber and Durkheim

TABLE 1.1 Methodology and research practice in Weber and Durkheim

	Weber *(1864–1920)*	*Durkheim* *(1858–1917)*
Methodology (principles)	*CMW/GAW* (1903–20)	*The Rules* (1895)
Empirical research (practice)	*The Protestant Ethic* (1904–5)	*Suicide* (1897)

do themselves'. In the case of Durkheim, I limit myself to *The Rules*, while my focus is on *CMW/GAW* in the case of Weber. As already mentioned, it is first and foremost in these works that one can expect to find their respective views on methodology. Concrete analyses from the pens of Weber and Durkheim – manifestations of their respective research practices and where it is possible to learn their craft in order to see 'what they actually do' – are primarily used to illustrate the relevance of methodological points and principles. Here, again, some concrete choices have been made.

In the case of Weber, I have chosen to concentrate on the posthumously published version of *The Protestant Ethic and the Spirit of Capitalism* (*Die protestantische Ethik und der Geist des Kapitalismus*), because this is among his most renowned works. Moreover, the two essays from 1904–5 were originally written at roughly the same time as that which is regarded as one of Weber's most important methodological works: 'The "Objectivity" of knowledge in social science and social policy' (*'Die "Objektivität" sozialwissenschaftlicher und sozialpolitischer Erkenntnis'*).

In the case of Durkheim, there are two obvious possibilities: *The Division of Labour in Society* and *Suicide*. Both works were written within a fairly short period of time in relation to *The Rules*. Here, I have chosen to stick to *Suicide* for several reasons. I think that *Suicide* supports one of the purposes behind *The Rules* more than *The Division of Labour in Society*; that is, to establish sociology as a scientific discipline. Furthermore, *Suicide* is much more of an empirical analysis than *The Division of Labour in Society*. And, in contrast to *The Division of Labour in Society*, it is advantageous to compare *Suicide* with Weber's *The Protestant Ethic* with respect to methodology.

I have largely chosen to use quotes from these four works in order to capture formulations in which Weber and Durkheim express themselves most clearly. This makes it possible to 'take a peek over their shoulders', so to speak. This also provides an impression of how they expressed themselves in their own words.[9] Again, this involves a somewhat 'naive' reading, as I have thus chosen to take the texts at face value. I thus refrain from attempting to read the texts symptomatically or trace who possibly inspired them. I make no attempt at determining who or what has formed the views of the two scholars. And there is no talk of investigating against whom they implicitly or explicitly are writing, assessing the extent to which they are in step with the spirit of their age, getting them to lie on the 'psychoanalyst's couch' or in any other manner attempting to 'get behind' the texts.

Aside from the fact that, in principle, it would be possible to devote numerous research careers to the collected works of Weber and Durkheim − and not least to all of the literature addressing their writings[10] − the approach and structure of the presentation chosen here must be understood in the context of the general purpose of the analysis as indicated in Table 1.1: to carry out a systematic, comparative analysis of Weber's and Durkheim's views on methodology in relation to a number of selected, basic dimensions. The analysis must then reveal how far it is possible to get by primarily restricting oneself to what are assumed to be the most important methodological works from their respective hands.[11]

In keeping with the interest in examining the methodological principles associated with research practice, I begin by considering the methodological principles reflected in *The Protestant Ethic* and *Suicide* (Chapter 2). I then address the methodological principles by analysing three main sets of fundamental questions. The first set is more or less related to matters of theory of science and epistemology and touches upon Weber's and Durkheim's respective 'social ontology' and their perspectives on the individual and society (Chapter 3); epistemological aspects in the form of their views on the subject–object problem in relation to the relationship between sociology and its object (Chapter 4); and the relationship between science and values (Chapter 5). The second main set is tied to the explanatory dimension, partly in relation to the question of methodological individualism (Chapter 6) and partly to the question of valid types of explanation (Chapter 7). The third and final main set of questions touches upon two associated matters: conceptual formation (Chapter 8) and laws (Chapter 9). In conclusion (Chapter 10), I briefly summarize the results of the analysis and return to Weber's and Durkheim's methodological views in the context of their respective research practices in *The Protestant Ethic* and *Suicide*. In relation to Table 1.1, I begin with the lowest horizontal level by addressing their research practices to see how they analyse, respectively, capitalism and suicide.

2

ANALYSING PROTESTANTS AND CATHOLICS

Suicide and *The Protestant Ethic* are used as examples of the research practices of Durkheim and Weber, as they provide a good taste of how the two scholars believe analyses are to be carried out in the social sciences. While suicide and capitalism are hardly the same phenomenon, the relationship between Protestantism and Catholicism plays a role in both *Suicide* and *The Protestant Ethic*. So, by being a little selective and directing the spotlight towards the significance of Protestantism and Catholicism in the two analyses, it becomes possible to draw comparisons revealing how differences in methodological principles are carried out in practice.

Durkheim: Protestants, Catholics – and suicide

On the basis of our everyday language and sense of awareness, Durkheim would surely be of the opinion that most people would feel that the concept of suicide does not require specific definition (*LS*: 1). Everybody knows what it refers to. And, as suicide is an individual act that is only of concern to the individual, one can well imagine that, in order to explain suicide, it is necessary to examine the intentions and life story of the individual leading up to the act; in so

10 Analysing Protestants and Catholics

doing, one would more or less regard suicide as a phenomenon that is a research area for psychology alone (*LS*: 8). However, Durkheim makes scientific, sociological claims that such perspectives do not hold. For example, the intentions of individuals are far too difficult to grasp: 'How discover the agent's motive and whether he desired death itself when he formed his resolve, or had some other purpose? *Intent is too intimate a thing to be more than approximately interpreted by another.* It even escapes self-observation' (*Suicide*: xli:).[1]

Moreover, the motives that – correctly or not – are attributed in statistics to those who commit also fail to reveal the true causes (*LS*: 144, 147). On the contrary, there is an alternative to the psychological approach to suicide, the sociological approach:

> If, instead of seeing in them only separate occurrences, unrelated and to be separately studied, the suicides committed in a given society during a given period of time are taken as a whole, it appears that *this total is not simply a sum of independent units, a collective total, but is itself a new fact,* sui generis, *with its own unity, individuality and consequently its own nature – a nature, furthermore, dominantly social.*
>
> (*Suicide*: xliv)[2]

Durkheim is not merely of the opinion that the suicides in a society in a specific period are a social phenomenon *sui generis*, but also that every society is predisposed to a certain number of voluntary deaths. The tendency towards suicide in a given society can be made the object of investigation for a specific study, and such study falls under sociological research activity. Naturally, Durkheim will carry out just such an investigation in *Suicide* (*LS*: 15).

How, more precisely, is such an investigation carried out? Using quantitative data as his preferred ammunition, Durkheim begins by shooting down various alternative explanations, including insanity, alcoholism, neurasthenia and imitation (*LS*: 19–138), in order to clear the road for his own explanations. Against that background, it is hardly surprising that Durkheim is of the opinion that a description of the individual case of suicide – no matter how good it may be – cannot say anything about which individual case has a sociological character

(*LS*: 143). Nor can sociologists fall back upon an everyday conceptualization of suicide, but must instead – as in the natural sciences – base their work on a general and precise definition of the phenomenon they intend to study. Towards this end, Durkheim discusses various ways of committing suicide, where the fundamental characterization of suicide is that the victim and perpetrator are one and the same person. Suicide can be carried out via what Durkheim refers to as a 'positive' act, i.e. an action such as the use of a firearm. It can be carried out 'negatively', i.e. by refraining from action, such as starving oneself to death. There is also a difference in the situations in which the suicide candidate has death as their direct intention, as opposed to cases in which there is a different purpose, but where the individual is well aware that the action will indirectly result in death. The latter can be the case of the soldier sacrificing himself for his regiment. Durkheim concludes that these ways of bringing about one's own death – positively or negatively, directly or indirectly – all share in common that the decisive action is carried out deliberately, the individual is aware of the consequences of their action, and this type of action subsequently forms a homogeneous cluster of deaths that can be distinguished from every other group of deaths. It can therefore also be referred to using a distinct word: suicide (*LS*: 1–5). Durkheim then presents his final definition of suicide: 'the term suicide is applied to all cases of death resulting directly or indirectly from a positive or negative act of the victim himself, which he knows will produce this result' (*Suicide*: xlii).[3]

Moreover: 'If one wants to know the several tributaries of suicide as a collective phenomenon one must regard it in its collective form, that is, through statistical data, from the start' (*Suicide*: 100).[4] Further distinction can be made between types of suicide in terms of the causes. According to Durkheim, in reality we can only talk about different types of suicide to the extent that their respective causes are different (*LS*: 141). At the same time, he is of the opinion that it is possible to ignore the individual's intentions and ideas and go directly to the causes. One must immediately enquire as to the state of the various social environments, such as the religious community, family, the political community, the professional community, etc., for which reason suicide varies (*LS*: 148).

12 Analysing Protestants and Catholics

This is what Durkheim proceeds to do. Durkheim believes that suicide can generally be divided into three main types according to cause: egoistic, altruistic and anomic suicide:

> *Egoistic suicide* results from man's no longer finding a basis for existence in life; *altruistic suicide*, because this basis for existence appears to man situated beyond life itself. The third sort of suicide, the existence of which has just been shown, results from man's activity's lacking regulation and his consequent sufferings. By virtue of its origin, we shall assign this last variety the name of *anomic suicide*.
>
> (*Suicide*: 219)[5]

Altruistic suicide, which Durkheim further subdivides in terms of obligatory, optional and acute suicide (*LS*: 233–46), occurs because society is excessively present in the individual; the individualization is too weak, and the integration is too strong. Anomic and egoistical suicides occur when the individual is too weakly integrated in society. Anomic suicide is typically associated with changes in society, crises and a lack of norms, which the individual can struggle to adapt to; conversely, egoistical suicide is a consequence of excessive individualism and inadequate integration (*LS*: 230, 271, 280–1, 288). And it is specifically in relation to the egoistical suicide type that Durkheim believes it is possible to observe an interesting causal relationship between suicide and confession of faith:

> If one casts a glance at the map of European suicide, it is at once clear that in purely Catholic countries like Spain, Portugal, Italy, suicide is very little developed, *while it is at its maximum in Protestant countries, in Prussia, Saxony, Denmark.*
>
> (*Suicide*: 105)[6]

According to Durkheim, it is possible to proceed to the presentation of a law based on a large number of observations: The frequency of suicide is simply proportional to the number of Protestants and inversely proportional to the number of Catholics. Thus, the frequency of suicide is relatively greater among Protestants than Catholics; moreover, it is also greater than among Jews, who consistently have the lowest suicide frequency of the three religions (*LS*: 152–4). But, by comparing the relative suicide frequency among Catholics and Protestants, Durkheim finds the following correlation: *Protestants are over-represented in relation to Catholics. Those are facts. How can they be explained?*

Here, according to Durkheim, it becomes necessary to examine the respective religious systems and their character. One of the differences between Protestantism and Catholicism is that the former permits more freedom of thought than the latter. However, this freedom of thought is merely the effect of a different, deeper condition that provides religion with a protective effect against suicide, but to a lesser extent for Protestantism than Catholicism:

> If religion protects man against the desire for self-destruction, it is not that it preaches the respect for his own person to him with arguments sui generis; *but because it is a society*. What constitutes this society is the existence of a certain number of beliefs and practices common to all the faithful, traditional and thus obligatory. *The more numerous and strong these collective states of mind are, the stronger the integration of the religious community, and also the greater its preservative value.* The details of dogmas and rites are secondary. *The essential thing is that they be capable of supporting a sufficiently intense collective life. And because the Protestant church has less consistency than the others it has less moderating effect upon suicide.*
> (*Suicide*: 125)[7]

Strictly speaking, it is not so much the content of the Protestant faith as much as it is the strength of the collective Protestant conceptions and customs that is of importance. Protestantism is weaker than the other religions and thus provides a lesser degree of integration of the individual in the Protestant society and a correspondingly higher risk of suicide among Protestants. Durkheim is of the opinion that it is possible to present the general proposition that the incidence of suicide varies inversely with the degree of integration in the religious community (*LS*: 222).

The explanation for a phenomenon that would otherwise appear to be as individual as suicide, is not to be found at the individual level:

14   Analysing Protestants and Catholics

'So true is it that suicide does not principally depend upon the congenital qualities of individuals but upon causes exterior to and dominating them!' (*Suicide*: 150).[8] In other words, the explanation is to be found in social conditions outside the individual that have bearing on the individual:

> *The conclusion from all these facts is that the social suicide-rate can be explained only sociologically.* At any given moment the moral constitution of society establishes the contingent of voluntary deaths. There is, therefore, for each people a collective force of a definite amount of energy, impelling men to self-destruction. The victim's acts which at first seem to express only his personal temperament *are really the supplement and prolongation of a social condition* which they express externally.
>
> This answers the question posed at the beginning of this work. It is not mere metaphor to say of each human society that it has a greater or lesser aptitude for suicide; the expression is based on the nature of things. Each social group really has a collective inclination for the act, quite its own, and the source of all individual inclination, rather than their result. It is made up of the currents of egoism, altruism or autonomy running through the society under consideration with the tendencies to languorous melancholy, active renunciation or exasperated weariness derivative from these currents. *These tendencies of the whole social body, by affecting individuals, cause them to commit suicide.*
>
> (*Suicide*: 263–4)[9]

Even though every society, according to Durkheim, is predisposed to a certain number of suicides, this does not stop him from ultimately considering whether the number of suicides constitutes an evil that can be reduced.[10] What is decisive here is whether the number of suicides can be regarded as normal or abnormal (*LS*: 413). Durkheim believes that there are a number of anomic and egoistical suicides in his time that are abnormal and almost sick. As a scientist, Durkheim must then propose a cure for the phenomenon, as science is the only available remedy against the malady (*LS*: 428, 171).

The cure with which Durkheim will fight this phenomenon consists first and foremost of allocating greater importance to vocational and professional associations or corporations (*LS*: 435–6). Durkheim believes that this will strengthen the individual's ties to society, such that the widespread egoistical and anomic suicides owing to inadequate integration in society can be reduced.

Against the background of this brief summary of a number of selected but central aspects of Durkheim's investigation into suicide, when considering his analysis, it becomes apparent that:

- Durkheim examines the individuals – or perhaps, rather, the individual – from the perspective of social conditions and not the other way around. In other words, he considers which social conditions drive individuals to suicide.
- Durkheim believes that the collective, social conditions pressing individuals to suicide have an objective existence and that an important explanatory factor of the various types of suicide is the degree of cohesion in society and in social groups.
- Durkheim places great emphasis on suicide representing a social relationship constituting an independent research area exclusively reserved for sociology as an independent scientific field and distinct from other fields of science, including contemporary psychology.
- Durkheim believes that it is possible to determine objectively the extent to which a phenomenon such as suicide is a social evil that sociology – in parallel with medical and biological approaches – can then contribute to diagnosing and preventing.
- Durkheim will not explain suicide on the basis of the intentions of individuals, but instead on the basis of causal factors, which cannot be reduced to the individual level.
- Durkheim establishes suicide as an object of investigation via a general conceptual determination.
- Durkheim does not consider it possible to capture a genuinely sociological phenomenon such as suicide via descriptions of individual cases.
- Durkheim perceives the challenge for sociology to be inductively establishing laws and regularities regarding the occurrence of suicide on the basis of empirical observations.

16 Analysing Protestants and Catholics

Keeping this characterization of these few selected features of Durkheim's approach in mind, it is instructive to consider now, briefly, how Weber analyses Protestants and Catholics.

Weber: Protestants, Catholics – and capitalism

Weber deals with Protestants and Catholics in an entirely different context from Durkheim. In a passing remark, he has since emphasized that his intention with the two articles on *The Protestant Ethic* was to study a complex and unique historical process: the breakthrough of Western, or modern, capitalism.[11] In order to do so, it is necessary to assume a particular perspective or point of view and highlight a number of decisive relationships in this process. Weber further emphasized that the two articles concentrate on the impact of religion on the economy – the relationship between the rational ethic of ascetic Protestantism and the modern, economic ethic – and he underlined that he is thus only investigating one side of this causal relationship (*DPE*: 21). Examining the impact of the economy on religion would require a different perspective.

More specifically, Weber bases his analysis in *The Protestant Ethic* on statistics for commerce in a number of European countries, including craftsmen, owners of capital and the self-employed. Here, he draws a conclusion that was well known in his day (*DPE*: 29–30): *Protestants are over-represented in relation to Catholics. Those are facts. How can they be explained?*

Weber casts a glance over history and points out that Protestant areas have also experienced greater economic prosperity than the Catholic-dominated regions. And, as opposed to Catholics, Protestants have displayed rational economic behaviour when the two groups have occupied comparable positions in society. In this connection, Weber rejects a couple of alternative explanations of this distinction between Protestantism and Catholicism, concluding that:

> *Thus the principal explanation of this difference must be sought in the permanent intrinsic character of their religious beliefs*, and not only in their temporary external historico-political situations . . .

Analysing Protestants and Catholics   17

> *It will be our task to investigate these religions with a view to finding out what peculiarities they have or have had which might have resulted in the behaviour we have described.*
>
> <div align="right">(<i>The Protestant Ethic</i>: 7)[12]</div>

As researcher, Weber wishes to examine the content, including the norms and values, of the religious views, regardless of whether or not he sympathizes with their content, and even though he is possibly of the opinion that the religious views have an illusive character. What is important here is that the religious norms and values have been overtaken by the individuals, that the individuals have subsequently adapted their behaviour accordingly, and that this behaviour has thus had causal effects.

Weber then constructs the first ideal type, referred to as the 'spirit of capitalism', which is also what he, in this context, calls a 'historical individual':

> i.e. a complex of elements associated in historical reality which we unite into a conceptual whole from the standpoint of their cultural significance.
>
> Such an historical concept, however, *since it refers in its content to a phenomenon significant for its unique individuality, cannot be defined according to the formula* genus proximum, differentia specifica, *but it must be gradually put together out of the individual parts which are taken from historical reality to make it up. Thus the final and definitive concept cannot stand at the beginning of the investigation, but must come at the end.* We must, in other words, work out in the course of the discussion, as its most important result, the best conceptual formulation of what we here understand by the spirit of capitalism, that is the best from the point of view which interests us here.
>
> <div align="right">(<i>The Protestant Ethic</i>: 13–14)[13]</div>

As to a more specific determination of the content of the spirit of capitalism, Weber refers to an individual historical phenomenon, which he claims to express this 'spirit' with almost classic purity: Benjamin Franklin's economic ethic (*DPE*: 40). Franklin's ethic

18 Analysing Protestants and Catholics

includes instructions as to how one ought to address others, be diligent and punctual, pay one's debts on time, allow one's money and oneself to work, and remember that time is money (*DPE*: 40–2). According to Weber, this economic ethic could only be found in the Western European/American form of capitalism and no other places in the world in which, according to Weber, capitalism also has existed. The most characteristic aspect of this ethic is that earning money is perceived as a calling, which is regarded as a goal in itself (*DPE*: 44–5). The subsequent spread and domination of capitalism and the market mechanism have meant that ways of life have been adapted to fit. The company owner or wage earner who fails to adapt to the norms of the market will go broke or become unemployed. But:

> In order that a manner of life so well adapted to the peculiarities of capitalism could be selected at all, i.e. should come to dominate others, *it had to originate somewhere, and not in isolated individuals alone, but as a way of life common to whole groups of men. This origin is what really needs explanation.*
>
> (*The Protestant Ethic*: 20)[14]

Weber is of the opinion that the source of this mentality, whereby profit and labour are understood as a calling, thus representing a break with the former, widespread traditional mentality, is to be found in the characteristics of Protestantism: early Calvinism. Weber then composes an entirely different ideal type: the ascetic Protestant calling ethic. Here, the emphasis is on those aspects of Calvinism that he understands as determining the behaviour of Calvinists in the sixteenth and seventeenth centuries. In other words, this ideal type cannot be found perfectly in the Calvinist reformation teachings, but it includes the aspects of Calvinism that are relevant from Weber's particular perspective.

Weber produces a lengthy account of the relevant aspects of Calvinism, the central aspect of which includes teaching about the omnipotence of God and selection for grace. God is inaccessible for people, who conversely only exist for God, and God has judged some people beforehand for salvation and others for eternal damnation (*DPE*: 121–2). This part of Calvinism has a consequence: 'In its extreme inhumanity this doctrine must above all have had one consequence for the life of a generation which surrendered to its magnificent consistency. That was *a feeling of unprecedented inner loneliness of the single individual*' (*The Protestant Ethic*: 60).[15] In other words, Weber considers the meaning and consequences that this teaching – in his opinion – must have had for the individual. Along these lines, he then asks:

> How was this doctrine borne . . . in an age to which the afterlife was not only more important, but in many ways also more certain, than all the interests of life in this world? . . . *The question, Am I one of the elect?, must sooner or later have arisen for every believer and have forced all other interests into the background. And how can I be sure of this state of grace?*
>
> (*The Protestant Ethic*: 65)[16]

Obviously, the Calvinist does not know the answer to this question, which Weber believed the individual Calvinists would pose to themselves. According to Weber, the Calvinist must therefore – for psychological reasons – seek a sign that he is among the chosen. Material prosperity is one such sign, which in the meantime should not distract one from the path of asceticism or the sense that one can be called to work (*DPE*: 131–2). As the Calvinist is seeking salvation but has no worldly evidence for it, the monastery moves out into society (*DPE*: 164–5). Individuals will feel God's watchful eye hanging over them around the clock, which precisely promotes ascetic behaviour with systematic and methodological work in the worldly life as a rational means for the achievement of the objective: a sign of salvation in the next life. So, work for God's sake – and your own! And Weber argued that this thinking – and the associated behaviour – had an impact in practice among Calvinists and the believers within the related Protestant denominations.

Weber then considers the relationship between the two ideal types and investigates the causal effects of a behaviour motivated by Calvinism and other variants of ascetic Protestantism on the capitalistic lifestyle and the economy, especially on consumption and production. He concludes that:

20 Analysing Protestants and Catholics

This worldly Protestant ascetism, as we may recapitulate up to this point, acted powerfully against the spontaneous enjoyment of possessions; *it restricted consumption*, especially of luxuries. On the other hand, it had the psychological effect of freeing the acquisition of goods from the inhibitions of traditionalistic ethics. *It broke the bonds of the impulse of acquisition* in that it not only legalized it, but (in the sense discussed) looked upon it as directly willed by God.

(*The Protestant Ethic*: 115)[17]

On the side of the production of private health, ascetism condemned both dishonesty and impulsive avarice. . . . And even more important: the religious valuation of restless, continuous, systematic work in a worldly calling, as the highest means to ascetism, and at the same time the surest and most evident proof of rebirth and genuine faith, must have been the most powerful conceivable lever for the expansion of that attitude toward life which we have here called the spirit of capitalism . . .

When the limitation of consumption is combined with this release of acquisitive activity, the inevitable practical result is obvious: accumulation of capital through ascetic compulsion to save. . . . The restraints which were imposed upon the consumption of wealth naturally served to increase it by making possible the productive investment of capital.

(*The Protestant Ethic*: 116)[18]

In other words, Weber believed that the call ethic of ascetic Protestantism probably contributed to the impact of capitalism by – as the psychological motivation for individuals, but on the collective level – provoking the formation of capital as an unintended causal effect of this behaviour.

Weber furthermore points out that, seen from the vantage point or the particular perspective that he developed in relation to the question regarding the significance of ascetic Protestantism for the historical breakthrough of capitalism, the religiously motivated effect of this behaviour can be distantly removed from both the insight and intent of Calvin and other reformers:

Analysing Protestants and Catholics   21

The salvation of the soul and that alone was the centre of their life and work. Their ethical ideal and the practical results of their doctrines were all based on that alone, and were the consequences of purely religious motives. We shall thus have to admit that *the cultural consequences of the Reformation were to a great extent, perhaps in the particular aspects with which we are dealing predominantly, unforeseen and even unwished-for results of the labours of the reformers.* They were often far removed from or even in contradiction to all that they themselves thought to attain.

(*The Protestant Ethic*: 48)[19]

Against the background of this brief summary of a number of selected, but important, aspects of how Weber carries out his analysis, it becomes apparent that:

- Weber views social relations on the basis of the perspective of the individual;
- Weber uses explanations based on meaning and intentions;
- Weber places emphasis on meaning and motives being decisive for the behaviour of groups of individuals;
- Weber looks for the causal effects of the behaviour and is aware that these effects are not necessarily in harmony with the motives determining the behaviour;
- in addition to intentional explanations, Weber also uses causal explanations;
- Weber does not use concepts à la *genus proximum et differentia specifica* in his investigation; and
- Weber will instead use ideal type concepts that are based on the emphasis of selected aspects of unique historical events.

Comparing and summarizing these features found in Weber's analysis with Durkheim's suicide analysis (cf. the section on Durkheim: Protestants, Catholics – and suicide, on p. 15), the differences between the two approaches to the empirical analyses are eye-catching. Although Durkheim and Weber both attempt to use causal explanations, the contrasts are conspicuous. For example, Weber uses ideal types in order to focus on unique events and conditions and, in that regard, rejects the use of generic concepts such as *genus proximum et differentia specifica*, which in practice are used by Durkheim in order to define and identify suicides as a subclass within the class of deaths. Weber draws on the content of the religion and the religious motives of the individuals as being essential to the explanation of the causal effects of the behaviour, whereas Durkheim rejects the use of intentional explanations and seeks to explain suicidal behaviour causally. Moreover, Weber sees social conditions from the perspective of the individual, whereas Durkheim sees the individual from the perspective of the social conditions.

My presentation of the two concrete analyses shows fundamental differences in Durkheim's and Weber's research activities that, in a consistent manner, are reflected in their respective methodological principles. In the following, I will systematically begin the study of such fundamental differences in Durkheim's and Weber's methodological principles by comparing them.

I begin with an examination of that which Durkheim and Weber each hold to be the significant characteristics of social life. In this connection, I simultaneously examine the perspective that they apply to understanding the relationship between society and the individual.

3

'SOCIAL ONTOLOGY'

Neither Weber nor Durkheim worked with social ontology, although their respective bodies of work both include assumptions and perceptions of what characterizes social reality and the relationship between the individual and society.[1] Their perceptions fit together with, and are decisive for, where and how they each draw the boundaries for the possibilities of producing knowledge of society.

Weber and Durkheim apply different perspectives on social reality and the individual–society relationship and end up with different conclusions against that background. With Weber, there is talk of a 'chaos perception', whereas it would be more accurate to talk of a 'cosmos perception' in the case of Durkheim. Moreover, Weber considers the society–individual relationship from the perspective of the individual, whereas Durkheim sees the same relationship from the perspective of society.

Weber: a chaos perception

> *The social science that we want to pursue is a science of reality. We want to understand the distinctive character of the reality of the life in which we are placed and which surrounds us –* on the one hand: the

24 'Social ontology'

> interrelation and the cultural significance and importance of its individual elements as they manifest themselves today; and, on the other: the reasons why the[se elements] historically developed as they did and not otherwise. *Now, as soon as we seek to reflect upon the way in which we encounter life in its immediate aspect, [we see that] it presents an absolutely infinite multiplicity of events 'within' and 'outside' ourselves, [events that] emerge and fade away successively and concurrently.*
>
> (*CMW/GAW*: 114)[2]

Weber wants to create an empirical science about the social or cultural reality. The '*Wirklichkeitswissenschaft*' – or science of reality – that he wants to bring about must account for the peculiar characteristics of the reality that the individual, and therefore also the researcher, is surrounded by and immersed within. Reality thus meets the individual and the researcher as an endless – and of itself almost chaotic – stream of events (*GAW*: 170–1, 184, 197, 203, 206–7, 213–14):

> *The immeasurable stream of events flows unendingly towards eternity.* The cultural problems that move humankind constantly assume new forms and colourings; within that *ever-infinite stream of individual events*, the boundaries of the area that acquires meaning and significance for us – which becomes a 'historical individual' – therefore remain fluid.
>
> (*CMW/GAW*: 121)[3]

Obviously, it would not be possible to obtain general knowledge about such a stream of events; such knowledge will always be partial. Even when taking a single event out of this eternally changing multiplicity, it would still not be possible to provide an exhaustive description of this event, and it is not possible to attain unconditional knowledge about reality. According to Weber, the only result from attempting to do so will be a chaos of 'existential judgements', that is, empirical statements. Despite reality having this character – or, more precisely formulated, the way reality meets us, according to Weber – it is nevertheless possible to attain scientific knowledge about this reality, and thereby also possible for science to avoid chaos:

'Social ontology'   25

The only reason why order can reign in that *chaos* is the fact that, in each case, it is only a part of individual reality that is of interest and has significance for us, because only that part has a relation to the cultural value ideas *with which we approach reality*.

(*CMW/GAW*: 118)[4]

This means that we must attempt to understand and explain reality on the basis of specific culturally based perspectives or points of view from which we analyse a selected segment of reality, so that: 'all knowledge of cultural reality is always knowledge from *specific and particular points of view*' (*CMW/GAW*: 119).[5]

The choice of which part of this chaotic multiplicity is to be made the object of scientific effort is determined by the individual's cultural values. The cultural values of the individual person cast light on the infinite multiplicity and colour or illuminate this specific segment of reality: '"Culture" is a finite section of *the meaningless infinity of events in the world*, endowed with meaning and significance *from a human perspective*' (*CMW/GAW*: 119).[6] The content of the cultural values will vary, but:

> The transcendental precondition of every cultural science is not that we find a particular, or indeed any, 'culture' valuable, but that we are *cultural beings, endowed with the capacity and the will to adopt a deliberate position with respect to the world, and to bestow meaning upon it.*
>
> (*CMW/GAW*: 119)[7]

All of the knowledge a researcher – and for that matter any other person – can obtain regarding the chaotic social or cultural reality has a transcendental condition, which thus runs prior to any possible experience, namely the possession of values. Social reality reveals itself as a unique and chaotic current of endless events, and cultural values thus have an impact on the perspective or point of view from which the individual person becomes interested in a segment of this current.

The above are social-ontological views that Weber does not argue for in greater detail, assuming them from others and attempting to apply them in a scientific context. As shown, he thus draws his own

26 'Social ontology'

conclusions regarding the possibilities for producing knowledge in the cultural sciences.

Weber clearly sees the world from the perspective of the *individual* and looks *out* at the world or social field immediately surrounding the individual in the form of a more or less chaotic multiplicity. The individual's cultural values and the perspective that the individual assumes illuminate segments of this chaotic field.

Durkheim: a cosmos perception

Like Weber, Durkheim is interested in creating a science about reality and, in this connection, Durkheim criticizes the point of view that it should be possible to create science by building on common sense or unsystematic data collected on an ad hoc basis. Nor do we get very far by merely further developing our own ideological conceptions and ideas about how things and our surroundings are linked together. Regardless of how useful such ideas possibly prove to be in practice, they are not to be elevated to science:

> By elaborating such [ideological, HJ] ideas in some fashion, one will therefore never arrive at *a discovery of the laws of reality*. On the contrary, they are like a veil drawn between the thing[s, HJ] and ourselves, concealing them from us the more successfully as we think them more transparent. Not only must such a science necessarily remain in a state of stagnation, but *it even lacks the materials upon which it might grow.*
>
> (*The Rules*: 15)[8]

In other words, reality is governed by laws that sociology can and must uncover, but sociology must have material from which it can seek and find nourishment. According to Durkheim, sociology has such material, and even has it all to itself. This material consists of the social facts, which Durkheim characterizes in the following manner: 'Here, then, is a category of facts with very distinctive characteristics: it consists of ways of acting, thinking, and feeling, *external to the individual*, and *endowed with a power of coercion, by reason of which they control him*' (*The Rules*: 3).[9] Durkheim justifies this characterization of the social facts as existing externally and having a compelling effect on the individual with the help of a thoroughly dualistic figure of argumentation. This consists of the individual being juxtaposed with society and the social facts. For example, a person of religious conviction finds their religious system to exist prior to their own birth. As the religious system exists *prior* to the believer, it also exists *outside* the believer. Correspondingly, a credit system or system of currency exists independently of whether or not an individual makes use of it (*LRLMS*: 4). At the same time, social facts also have a coercive impact on the behaviour and consciousness of the individual. As with things, Durkheim reasons that social facts cannot be influenced by pure acts of willpower. On the contrary, they make their presence felt if the individual attempts to resist them. Should the individual violate the law, they will – depending on how far they get in the attempt – be met by measures aimed at preventing the action in question, restoring past conditions or punishing the individual. Should an individual attempt to socialize with their compatriots without making use of their shared national language or without using the conventional means of payment, their attempt will fall flat. The individual will be pressured to succumb to the social facts and conform to the behaviour of their compatriots. The social facts have objective existence and force the behaviour and consciousness of the individual in specific directions. According to Durkheim, the social facts constitute a reality *sui generis* (*LRLMS*: 5, 9) and exist independently of their individual manifestations. That renders them well suited to observation for sociology, as they are stable regardless of whether or not society undergoes gradual change:

> *Social life consists, then, of free currents perpetually in the process of transformation* and incapable of being mentally fixed by the observer, and the scholar cannot approach the study of social reality from this angle. But we know that *it possesses the power of crystallization without ceasing to be itself.* Thus, apart from the individual acts to which they give rise, collective habits find expression in definite forms: legal rules, moral regulations, popular proverbs, social conventions, etc. As *these forms have a permanent existence and do not change with the diverse applications made*

28 'Social ontology'

> *of them, they constitute a fixed object*, a constant standard within the observer's reach, exclusive of subjective impressions and purely personal observations.
>
> (*The Rules*: 45)[10]

As presented here, society has characteristics that make it possible for the sociologist to produce scientific cognition and objective knowledge. But Durkheim does not stop here. Society also has characteristics that, on a scientific basis, enable sociology, if necessary, to change and improve the state of society, because, like an organism, society can be healthy or ill: 'Briefly, *for societies* as for individuals, *health is good and desirable*; *disease*, on the contrary, *is bad* and to be avoided' (*The Rules*: 49).[11]

In continuation of these social-ontological considerations regarding the characteristics of society and social life, one can say in summary that, according to Durkheim, society and the social facts are characterized as having objective existence; society contains social facts, structures and laws, and shares features in common with an organism, and there are indeed associated possibilities for attaining insight into these features in society. The insights become apparent to those who are able to set aside their conventional ideas and conceptions and see society through Durkheim's perspective.

Against that background and in summary, there is reason to conclude that Durkheim, unlike Weber, definitely does not mean to look into a chaos, but rather into a cosmos. And, as opposed to Weber, Durkheim generally applies a perspective of society and the individuals – or rather, *the* individual – where, in the juxtaposition of society and the individual, he sees this relationship from the *perspective of society and the social facts*. In general, Durkheim registers *from the outside* how society and social facts have a coercive impact on the behaviour and psychological state of the individual.

It might be possible to compare the social-ontological elements in Weber's and Durkheim's characterizations of society and the individual's relations to society using an anthill analogy. Durkheim notes how the individual ant is born into an ant colony that existed before the birth of the ant and will continue to exist after its death. The individual ant will never be able to move the anthill. Instead, it is forced

'Social ontology' 29

to adapt and move along the tunnels in the anthill. At the same time, the anthill is an organism that is gradually changing. It has built-in, stable structures that ensure its survival, which is in part owing to how the ants contribute to its maintenance. In contrast, Weber sees society and the positioning of the individual within it in a manner akin to seeing the anthill from the perspective of the individual ant. Each ant is directed by its own activities, which imbue its relations to its surroundings with meaning, and it moves around the tunnels of the anthill and its hollow spaces. The ant is constantly met by the parts of the anthill that do not remain in the dark as a chaos of changing lights and colours, of surroundings that are under construction and demolition, and of other ants busy doing the same or different things. To the extent that several ants engage in the same activities, these can result in the anthill changing – intentionally or unintentionally – and thus developing new tunnels and hollow spaces.

Leaving this analogy and considering the social-ontological elements in Weber and Durkheim emphasized here, they are visibly connected by epistemological points of view. Aspects of social reality and other aspects of reality have consequences for our possibilities for producing true knowledge about the very same social reality. Here, Weber primarily places these possibilities on the side of the subject. The ever-changing multiplicity in which reality, according to Weber, meets the researcher does not exclude the production of scientific knowledge. Man is a cultural being, endowed with the prerequisites to produce knowledge, albeit within specific boundaries. Conversely, Durkheim is inclined to place the possibilities for producing scientific knowledge on the side of the object. Even though society consists of constantly shifting streams, streams that the researcher's gaze cannot hold still, society is still crystallized in stable forms that constitute a constant object. This object is within the grasp of the researcher. Using the correct method, the object can, in principle, be researched free of limitations in the form of the subjective or personal distortion of the results.

The next chapter will support how, in relation to this subject–object question, we find the differences indicated in Weber's and Durkheim's epistemological views.

4
EPISTEMOLOGY

In this chapter, I will address selected epistemological aspects of Durkheim's and Weber's methodologies. I do this first by examining how they approach the subject–object problem in the form of the relationship between sociology (the subject) and its object of study. In Durkheim and Weber alike, it is possible to find two rather significant criteria for scientific discipline autonomy, namely the requirements regarding an independent object or a particular approach to the same. Despite this similarity, they have rather different views on the relationship between sociology and its object. Next, there is occasion to examine a number of other epistemological aspects. Durkheim, who on some points has inductivism-oriented views, sets further limits regarding the sociological possibilities for producing knowledge than does Weber, whose influences include neo-Kantianism.

Durkheim: inductivism

For Durkheim, it is the assertion of an independent object of its own that can – and shall – legitimize the status of sociology as an autonomous scientific discipline. As opposed to Weber, whose early writings distance him from the label 'sociology' (*GAW*: 11, 48) and focus on

Epistemology   31

the cultural sciences, *The Rules* is about a 'founding project'. *The Rules* can be read as an attempt at founding or establishing a scientific discipline, sociology, which is an independent and autonomous discipline on the same level as the psychology of the day and other sciences. In the conclusion of *The Rules*, Durkheim thus writes that his endeavour has been to establish or institute a scientific discipline (*LRLMS*: 141). And, as regards this project, Durkheim concludes in the same breath that:

> Sociology is, then not an auxiliary of another science; *it is itself a distinct and autonomous science*, and the feeling of the specificity of social reality is indeed so necessary to the sociologist that only distinctly sociological training can prepare him to grasp social facts intelligently.
>
> (*The Rules*: 145)[1]

The basic assumption for sociology possibly being a distinct and autonomous scientific discipline is that it has an object of its own, which other sciences are unable to investigate. This is the *raison d'être* of sociology (*LRLMS*: 6, 143). It is, therefore, also important for Durkheim to delineate the object of sociology in such a manner that it cannot be reduced to an object for other scientific disciplines. As such, he distinguishes sociology from neighbouring disciplines such as the psychology of his day (*LRLMS*: 30–1, 100–1, 142–3). The object of sociology is the social facts, which are real and exist in their own right (cf. the section in Chapter 3 on Durkheim: a cosmos perception), and which, in Durkheim's words, constitute a reality *sui generis* in society.

Durkheim's rule about considering social facts as things (*LRLMS*: 15) is understandable against this background, even though he is not entirely clear on this point. Without being things, social facts have the same ontological status as material things, in the sense that they also have objective existence. Durkheim's arguments to this end include the point that social facts – in addition to having a coercive impact upon the behaviour of the individual – are in keeping with the claim that things exist outside the individual and are therefore not affected by the individual's will (*LRLMS*: 3–14). By the same token, social facts

32 Epistemology

do not have the same epistemological status as material things, but they can be expressed and observed through things. As such, the sociologist can attain access to them independently of the ideas that the individuals have about them. For example, the court is expressed through books on law, and fashion through clothing (*LRLMS*: 27–8, 30). As the first step towards a characterization of Durkheim's perception of the subject–object relationship that the discipline of sociology has as its object, there is thus talk of sociology having an exclusive research object, an object that other scientific disciplines do not deal with. It consists of social facts. They have objective existence, and in that sense they constitute a real object. Strictly speaking, the object of sociology is merely waiting for a subject – sociology and the sociologists – to investigate it. In establishing the relationship that sociology as a discipline has to its object of research, Durkheim thus places emphasis on the object side of this relationship.

One may then ask what the possibilities are for producing scientific knowledge regarding this object. On this point, there is at the same time a relatively strong, although not entirely unambiguous, tendency in Durkheim to believe that sociology and the sociologist are able to obtain unbiased or 'pure' access to the object of research. Durkheim thus asserts that, even though social facts are not directly observable, it is possible to observe them in their pure form by making certain 'moves' or using certain devices (*LRLMS*: 9). This points in the same direction as when he claims, for example, that:

> Since objects are perceived only through sense perception, we can conclude: *Science, to be objective, ought to start, not with concepts formed independent to them, but with these same perceptions.* . . . From sensation all general ideas flow, whether they be true or false, scientific or impressionistic. *The point of departure of science, or speculative knowledge, cannot be different from that of lay, or practical knowledge. It is only beyond this point, namely, in the manner of elaboration of these common data, that divergences begin.*
>
> (*The Rules*: 43–4)[2]

This points towards a belief that sociology, in principle, is able to gain 'pure' access to its object via a combination of sensory perception

Epistemology 33

and an adequate processing of the sensory impressions that is part of Durkheim's epistemology. This epistemology also includes elements of inductivism, which render it possible and desirable both to attain certain knowledge via observations and to make valid generalizations on the basis of a finite number of observations, that is, via induction. These elements of inductivism are found in Durkheim, although not completely unambiguously. Thus, according to Durkheim, science is characterized as being based on sensory perceptions and observations. By processing the observations scientifically and correctly, it becomes possible to obtain knowledge regarding the object. It can also be understood in this light when the sociologist, in order to be scientific, not only has to consider the social facts as things, but must also eradicate all preconceptions before beginning scientific investigation. This prevents the preconceptions from interfering with the observation and cognition of the things and the social facts themselves (*LRLMS*: 16, 23–4, 31). Moreover, Durkheim is pulling in the same direction when, as an argument for classifying groups of phenomena according to the outward characteristics they share in common, he asserts that:

> By proceeding thus, the sociologist, from the very first, is *firmly grounded in reality*. Indeed, the pattern of such a classification does not depend on him or on the cast of his individual mind *but on the nature of things*.
>
> (*The Rules*: 36)[3]

Finally, and well in line with the ideal of inductivism, the establishment of laws through induction is a deep-rooted ideal for Durkheim. For instance, he criticizes economists for considering the 'law' of supply and demand a law, despite the fact that it has not been established inductively (*LRLMS*: 26). In a debate about comparative method and the sociological application of data material, Durkheim correspondingly claims that: 'As soon as one has proved that, in a certain number of cases, two phenomena vary with one another, one is *certain* of being in the presence of a law' (*The Rules*: 133).[4]

As the second step in a characterization of Durkheim's ambition of founding sociology as a science and the associated view on the subject–object relationship between sociology and its object, one might

34 Epistemology

say that parts of his epistemology contain elements of inductivism and that he strikes a rather positive note regarding the possibilities for gaining true sociological knowledge. These possibilities are not totally unlimited, however, as Durkheim also states that the human mind may possibly never grasp the social reality completely (*LRLMS*: 46).

Weber: neo-Kantianism

The 'late' Weber views himself as representing an 'interpretive sociology', thereby explicitly accepting the 'sociology' label. Here, Weber implicitly shares Durkheim's conviction that an independent scientific discipline – therein, also sociology – must possess its own object. Considering Weber's early methodological writings, it seems as though this criterion is being supplemented by – or is almost secondary in relation to – the criterion of a unique and independent approach to the object.

Like Durkheim, the late Weber thus places emphasis on delimiting the object of sociology. Unlike Durkheim, however, Weber chooses to make meaningful social behaviour the primary object of sociology: 'For sociology in the sense used here, as for history, the object under consideration is the *meaning with which behaviour is endowed*' (*BSC/ GAW*: 320).[5]

This point of view is also found elsewhere (*GAW*: 429, 547): 'Sociology is not only concerned with "social action"; *for the sociology pursued here this is simply its central referent*, what could be said to be *constitutive for it as a science*' (*BSE/GAW*: 329).[6]

For Weber, as opposed to Durkheim, this constitution of the object of sociology is based more in the approach to the object. Consequently, where Durkheim emphasizes the object side of the subject–object relationship, Weber stresses the subject side of the relationship. This becomes clear in connection with Weber's discussion and determination of what characterizes social economy, not sociology, and in that context what is to be understood as being 'social economic':

> However, the quality of an event as a 'social-economic' phenomenon is not something that is 'objectively' inherent in it. Instead, *it is determined by the direction of our cognitive interest*

Epistemology   35

resulting from the specific cultural significance that we, in each case, attach to the event in question.

(*CMW/GAW*: 108–9)[7]

In other words, Weber is emphasizing how 'the social economic' is not something that sticks to the research object of the discipline '*an sich*', but rather depends on the researcher's culturally conditioned cognitive interest. The determination of the object is thus pre-conditioned by the subject and depends on the researcher's perspective or approach to the object:

> The fields of inquiry of scientific disciplines are based *not on 'concrete' relations between 'things', but on 'theoretical' relations between 'problems'*: when new methods are used to investigate a new problem, and this leads to the uncovering of truths that open up new, significant perspectives, then a new 'science' comes into being.
>
> (*CMW/GAW*: 111)[8]

Weber elaborates on this point in several ways and in several different contexts, using the murder of Caesar as an example. Here, the same phenomenon, the murder of Caesar, will be investigated from a number of different perspectives and different cognitive interests. For the judge or legal dogmatist, what is interesting is whether a specific action falls within a judicial norm. Conversely, historians or physicians will study the phenomenon from entirely different perspectives (*GAW*: 272–3).

Further along these lines, there is yet another difference between the views found in Durkheim and Weber on the relationship between sociology and its object. For Weber, there is more talk of an object of knowledge as opposed to a real object, to which the sociologist is alleged to have unbiased access. Weber explicitly criticizes the view that it is possible, in principle, for a science to gain 'pure' access to a real object:

> Consequently, *all knowledge of cultural reality is always knowledge from specific and particular points of view.* When we demand of historians and social scientists, as an elementary prerequisite, that

36 Epistemology

they must be able to distinguish between what is important and what is unimportant, and that they must possess the 'points of view' necessary for making that distinction, this simply means that they must be able – consciously or unconsciously – to relate what happens in [empirical] reality to universal 'cultural values', and, on that basis, to select those relationships which are significant for us. *Again and again, the notion crops up that such perspectives can be 'derived from the material itself'; but this is owing to a naïve self-deception on the part of academic specialists* who do not realize that they have unconsciously, from the very beginning, approached their material with value ideas on the basis of which they have then selected a tiny part of an absolute infinity, as being all that they are concerned with observing. . . .

The search for knowledge in the field of the cultural sciences (in our sense) is therefore tied to 'subjective' preconditions insofar as it is only concerned with those parts of reality that are – however indirectly – connected with occurrences to which we attach cultural significance.

(*CMW/GAW*: 119–20)[9]

Even though the quote only touches upon a limited element of Weber's epistemology, namely neo-Kantianism, it must be assumed to contribute to Weber here being of the opinion that the researcher will, in principle, never be able to gain pure access to the object. In other words, he does not strike epistemological tones that are anywhere close to being as positive as Durkheim. Entirely in the spirit of Kant, Weber places limitations on the possibilities of gaining knowledge on the side of the subject. This is well in line with the earlier finding (cf. the section in Chapter 3 on Weber: a chaos perception) that the transcendental precondition for any cultural science is, according to Weber, that we are cultural beings who are endowed with the prerequisites to take deliberate positions with respect to the world and give it meaning. Weber's analysis in 'The "Objectivity" of knowledge in social sciences and social policy' can thus also be read in part as a more or less Kantian analysis of the conditions for producing knowledge in the cultural sciences. And Kantian views are similarly expressed when Weber writes:

> *There is and remains* – and this is what matters to us – *an eternal, unbridgeable difference* as to whether an argument is aimed at our feelings and our capacity for embracing with enthusiasm concrete practical goals, or forms and elements of culture; or, if it is a question concerning the validity of ethical norms, [whether it is aimed at] our conscience; or finally, [whether it is aimed] at our ability and need to order empirical reality intellectually in a manner that claims validity as empirical truth.
>
> (*CMW/GAW*: 105)[10]

An empirical science produces knowledge and truth via the human ability to order empirical reality intellectually. There is an unbridgeable divide between statements that are directed to feelings and the conscience as opposed to statements directed at reason. In Kantian terms, there is a difference between '*Sollen*' and '*Sein*'. And, in non-Kantian terms, which Weber also uses on occasion, there is a difference between the empirical and the normative (*GAW*: 32, 157, 160, 343).

As the next chapter will show, Weber also distances himself from Durkheim with respect to the question about the capacity of science to deal with values. Again, Weber is more of an epistemological pessimist than Durkheim.

5
SCIENCE AND VALUES

Weber and Durkheim both formulate views on the question regarding the capacity of science to deal with values. This is narrowly associated with the question concerning the relationship between 'Is' and 'Ought'. This is also referred to in terms of descriptive versus normative statements, empirical propositions versus value judgements, the '*Sein–Sollen*' dilemma, the 'naturalistic' fallacy, etc. Weber is explicit in his treatment of, and view on, values. The theme pops up repeatedly in his works. Durkheim, on the other hand, deals with the question more implicitly, addressing it in the context of a discussion of normal versus pathological social facts. And, once again, we see Weber drawing narrower limits for producing knowledge and dealing with values than Durkheim.

Weber: the gulf between 'Is' and 'Ought'

It has already been described how Weber has the absolute basic position that every individual is part of a specific culture and that their relationship to the world around them is coloured by values (cf. the section in Chapter 3 on Weber: a chaos perception). This also goes for researchers in the social sciences. In this manner, the research process will always be impacted by values (cf. the section in Chapter 4 on Weber: neo-Kantianism). For example, the choice and establishment of a specific research object and the perspective through which researchers examine the research object will be value-related:

> There is no absolutely 'objective' scientific analysis of cultural life – or (to use a term which is perhaps somewhat narrower but which, for our purposes, does not have an essentially different meaning) of 'social phenomena' – independent of special and 'one-sided' points of view, according to which [those phenomena] are – explicitly or implicitly, deliberately or unconsciously – selected as an object of inquiry, analysed and presented in an orderly fashion.
>
> (CMW/GAW: 113)[1]

Weber combines this view on the considerable significance of values with another perception of values, as presented before (cf. the section in Chapter 4 on Weber: neo-Kantianism), namely that there is an insurmountable gulf between empirical propositions and value judgements. This massive divide subsequently excludes value judgements from being inferred from empirical analysis. For example, in criticism of Wundt, a contemporary German psychologist who graduated in medicine, Weber claims that:

> It would go too far if we were now also, after this laborious account of 'self-evident [truths]', to discuss the fact that precisely the same is true for other values than that of striving for scientific knowledge. There is absolutely no bridge that leads from a purely 'empirical' analysis of given reality with the tools of causal explanation to establishing or contesting the 'validity' of any value judgement; and Wundt's concepts of 'creative synthesis', of the 'law' of constant 'intensification of psychical energy' etc. contain value judgements of the first water.[2]
>
> (CMW/GAW: 40)

Even though maintaining the distinction between empirical propositions and value judgements, or between 'Is' and 'Ought', is entirely fundamental in Weber's work (GAW: 32, 61, 146, 148, 160,

40   Science and values

199, 225, 313, 343, 358, 421, 501, 523, 557, 602), in *CMW/GAW*, he at best only hints at how the distinction should be drawn. He merely hints (cf. the section in Chapter 4 on Weber: neo-Kantianism) at the distinction between argumentation that, on the one side, appeals to feelings and conscience and argumentation that, on the other side, addresses our ability and desire to use the force of our intellect to order the empirical reality in a manner that raises demands regarding validity and empirical truth (*GAW*: 155, 157). Aside from this discreet salute to Kant, Weber merely refers anyone interested in a more detailed account of the content of the distinction between 'Is' and 'Ought' to the neo-Kantian logicians of his time (*GAW*: 146). Instead, Weber concentrates on drawing consequences from the assumption about the distinction between 'Is' and 'Ought'. The consequences he draws also imply that he is, at the same time, seeking to maintain the view that the research process is inherently marked by values, and to avoid landing in subjectivism, where cognition and knowledge are laid bare by subjective values.

First, Weber claims that, if the scientific approach has been methodologically correct, then, in principle, the validity of the research results cannot be challenged. They will be compelling, also for someone born into a different culture or merely holding other cultural values:

> For it is, and continues to be, true that a methodically correct proof in the field of social science must, in order to have reached its goal, also be accepted as correct even by a Chinese – or, to put it more correctly: that goal must at any rate be striven for, although it may not be completely attainable because the data are lacking. In the same way, moreover, the logical analysis of an ideal with respect to its contents and its ultimate axioms, and the demonstration of the logical and practical consequences of pursuing this ideal, must also, if it is to be deemed successful, be valid for [a Chinese]. Even though he may not be 'attuned' to our ethical imperatives, and even though he may, and most probably often will, reject the ideal and the concrete valuations flowing from it, this in no way detracts from the scientific value of that intellectual analysis.

(*CMW/GAW*: 105)[3]

Science and values   41

Second, empirical social science is not prevented from analysing the values and goals of others. This can be carried out in different ways, based on ends–means thinking. According to Weber, this is the fundamental basis for understanding people's meaning-bearing actions. The social scientist can provide another person with knowledge and awareness about the significance of the individual's values and goals by assessing whether the values and goals are internally consistent. The social scientist can also take a position regarding the question as to whether the means are well suited to realizing a given goal. Further along these lines, and to the extent that the means lead to the end, the researcher can also assume a position regarding the unintended consequences of the means in the light of other goals and values for the person in question. This means that the social scientist can assess the 'costs' the person in question might have to 'pay' at some point in order to put means to use that might well fulfil one goal but that, at the same time, have unforeseen consequences if their use is at odds with other goals and values (*GAW*: 149–51); and values typically clash with one another.

This context renders Weber's distinction between an ethic of conviction and an ethic of responsibility relevant. An ethic of conviction entails maintaining a goal or specific values regardless of the consequences of the actions aimed at advancing the goal and values. An ethic of responsibility entails other goals and values being drawn upon and considered in the light of the expected consequences of the specific actions (*GAW*: 505).

Making ethical or value-oriented decisions on behalf of others, or assessing another person's basic values in ways other than those described here, would be outside the realm of empirical science. For example, a social scientist cannot choose goals or values on behalf of others; everyone must choose and decide for themselves: 'An empirical science cannot tell someone what he ought to do, but *only* what he can do and – possibly – what he wants to do' (*CMW/GAW*: 103).[4] Social scientists may make value judgements; strictly speaking, however, not in their capacity as scientists:

> Everyone is free, even in the form of a historical account, to assert himself as a 'subject taking a stand', to propagate political

42 Science and values

or cultural ideals or other 'value judgements', and to make use of the whole material of history to illustrate the practical importance of those ideals, or of those that he fights against. In the same way, biologists or anthropologists introduce certain very subjective ideals of 'progress', or philosophical convictions, into their investigations; in so doing, they are of course acting no differently from someone who perhaps employs the whole panoply of knowledge furnished by the natural sciences as an edifying illustration of the 'grace of God'. But *in every such case, it is not the scholar, but the evaluating human being who speaks, and his exposition is aimed, not only at subjects who seek theoretical knowledge, but [also] at those who make value judgements.*

(*CMW/GAW*: 58)[5]

Weber does not rule out social scientists formulating value judgements marked by their own ideals, but doing so imposes obligations on the individual scholar. First, social scientists must clarify their own ideals and standards when assessing the practical or political ideals of others, for example, as part of a social-policy debate on legislation (*GAW*: 156–7). Weber regards the second obligation to be a consequence of the first, namely that social scientists must constantly make it clear for their readers, as well as themselves, when it is no longer the reasoning scholar but rather the striving human being who is speaking. In Weber's Kantian-inspired terminology, scholars must maintain a level of self-awareness in terms of when arguments are addressed to reason and when they address feelings; scholars must avoid mixing the scientific analysis of fact with value judgements (*GAW*: 156–7): '*What the criticism in the preceding remarks is aimed at is this [practice of] mixing-up*, but certainly not standing up for, one's own ideals. Lack of conviction has no inherent affinity whatsoever to scientific "objectivity"' (*CMW/GAW*: 106).[6]

Moreover, Weber also sends out strong warnings against believing that it should be at all possible to formulate positions on values on an objective scientific foundation owing to the fact that the position is situated between two political extremes: 'What must be *combated with the greatest possible determination* is the idea (which is not infrequently met with) that one can come closer to scientific "objectivity" by

Science and values   43

weighing the different valuations against each other and [finding] a
"statesmanlike" compromise' (*CMW/GAW*: 310).[7]

In other words, Weber sees the political 'middle course' as being no
closer to objectivity and the scientific truth than the most extreme party
ideals on the left or right. In order to protect the interests of science, it
is necessary to recognize these inconvenient facts (*GAW*: 154–5).

Thus, scholars necessarily have ideals and values inasmuch as they
are born into a specific culture. However, neither this fact nor the
insurmountable gulf between 'Is' and 'Ought' deprives them of the
possibilities for producing valid empirical knowledge, although these
are hardly unlimited. An empirical science cannot tell anyone anything
about which values they ought to hold dear, nor which goals they
ought to pursue.

Durkheim: the bridge between 'Is' and 'Ought'

Durkheim, who leaves little space for the value issue in *The Rules*,
actually proceeds beyond Weber in his view on the capacity of
science to deal with value judgements. Durkheim thus holds that it
is possible to distinguish between two kinds of phenomenon when
making observations: 'those which conform to given standards and
those which "ought" to be different – in other words, normal and
pathological phenomena' (*The Rules*: 47).[8]

Next, Durkheim raises the question as to whether science can carry
out this distinction between 'Is' and 'Ought'. Like Weber, Durkheim
finds this to be the case. However, he does not stop at raising this as
a view in principle, going beyond Weber and outlining how this
distinction is to be carried out in practice.

Durkheim's distinction between 'the phenomena that are as they
should be and those that are not as they ought to be' implies that he
is of the opinion that it is possible, one way or another, to distinguish
between 'Is' and 'Ought'. This view becomes apparent in his criticism
of how a number of economists and moral philosophers analyse societal
relations. They build their conclusions on the basis of abstract
speculation, which they conveniently spice up with a few affirmative
examples. Instead, they ought to be going about their work in a
conscientious and inductive manner. Moreover:

44 Science and values

even these abstract speculations do not constitute a science, strictly speaking, since their object is the determination *not of that which is*, in fact, the supreme rule of morality *but of what ought to be*. Similarly, economists are today principally occupied with the problem of whether society *ought* to be organized on an individualistic or socialistic basis, whether it is *better* that the state should intervene in industrial and commercial relations, or whether it is *better* to abandon them to private initiative; whether one *ought* to use a single monetary standard, or a bimetallic system, etc. It contains few laws in the proper sense of the word; even what are commonly called 'laws' are generally unworthy of this designation since *they are merely maxims for action, or practical precepts in disguise. The famous law of supply and demand, for example, has never been inductively established, as should be the case with a law referring to economic reality*.

(*The Rules*: 26)[9]

Had economists gone about their work in a systematic manner, then they would have formulated laws expressing actual relationships on an inductive basis, as opposed to how they would like them to be (*LRLMS*: 27).

However, Durkheim's criticism is not a criticism as to principles in the sense that he condemns normative elements as such in analyses. The problem is rather that the value judgements made by economists and moral philosophers appear excessively unmediated and immediate, and that they are made on excessively shaky foundations. While Durkheim understands the primary responsibility of science as describing and analysing actual relations, he criticizes those who will limit their efforts to do this:

According to a theory whose partisans belong to most diverse schools, *science can teach us nothing about what we ought to desire*. It is concerned, they say, only with facts which all have the same value and interest for us; it observes and explains, but does not judge them. Good and evil do not exist for science. *It can, indeed, tell us how given causes produce their effects, but not what ends should be pursued*.

(*The Rules*: 47)[10]

Durkheim argues further that science would risk losing an important reason for its existence if it were to refrain from making statements about the goals that ought to be pursued: '*Science thus loses all, or almost all, practical effectiveness and, consequently, its principal justification for existence.* Why strive for knowledge of reality if this knowledge cannot serve us in life?' (*The Rules*: 48).[11] In other words, science is close to being worthless if it does not guide behaviour and is not practically applicable. In this connection, Durkheim formulates his view on the opportunity to deal scientifically with ends and means in a manner that Weber would dismiss:

> *If science cannot indicate the best goal to us, how can it inform us about the best means to reach it?* Why should it recommend the most rapid in preference to the most economical, the surest rather than the simplest, or vice versa? *If science cannot guide us in the determination of ultimate ends, it is equally powerless in the case of those secondary and subordinate ends called 'means'.*
>
> (*The Rules*: 48)[12]

Not only is Durkheim of the opinion that sociology can assume a position regarding the establishment of the highest goals, thereby delivering value judgements in the Weberian sense, without losing its scientific objectivity, he argues further that science is able to indicate how this can be done.

Here, Durkheim chooses a basic value that he believes everyone shares: an interest in health. He finds that it is possible to transfer this from individuals to society using an organism analogy:

> Briefly, *for societies as for individuals, health is good and desirable; disease, on the contrary, is bad and to be avoided.* If, then, we can find an *objective criterion, inherent in the facts themselves,* which enables us to distinguish scientifically between health and morbidity in the various orders of social phenomena, science will be in a position to throw light on practical problems and still remain faithful to its own method.
>
> (*The Rules*: 49)[13]

46 Science and values

In other words, if it is possible to ascertain objective criteria that can ultimately enable science to draw a distinction between 'normal' and 'pathological', then Durkheim no longer sees any insurmountable divide: 'There is no longer a gulf between science and art; but on the contrary there is [no, HJ] break of continuity between them' (*The Rules*: 49).[14] This is yet another claim that Weber would reject. For Durkheim, however, the question then becomes whether it is possible, in practice and principle alike, to find an objective criterion for health. He argues this to be the case.

After rejecting pain and probabilities of survival as criteria, he arrives at a distinction between the normal, understood as healthy, and the pathological, understood as illness, which can be coupled together with a number of conditions regarding the dissemination of a phenomenon and with the concept 'average type'. Drawing a parallel to biology, Durkheim emphasizes that what is normal for one species is not necessarily normal for another. A phenomenon can only be regarded as pathological within a given species, and the conditions of health and illness cannot be established on an abstract level. Here, he criticizes what he regards as being an excessively widespread tendency to judge a social fact as though it were good or bad, in and by itself. Instead, the average type should be taken into consideration, together with a distinction in terms of the type of society the social fact exists in, how widespread it is, and which phase of development it is in. By placing emphasis on such factors, Durkheim is of the opinion that it is possible to assess whether a social fact is normal or pathological.

Durkheim also refers to a secondary method to this end, which is to consider whether the previous conditions for the existence of the normal phenomenon remain present, as this must at the same time be general. By following this method, the sociologist is then all the more able to tell if the social fact is normal or pathological (*LRLMS*: 55–64).

The perspective for the use of such methods is that it becomes possible to engage in political action and make political decisions on a scientific basis, neither more nor less:

> The duty of the statesman is no longer to push society toward an ideal that seems attractive to him, but *his role is that of the*

Science and values 47

physician: he prevents the outbreak of illnesses by good hygiene, and he seeks to cure them when they have appeared.

(*The Rules*: 75)[15]

According to Durkheim's methodology, it is thus possible, both in principle and practice, to pass value judgements about social facts by making inferences from observations and factual findings of the normal or pathological character of a social fact. Durkheim would thus appear to be of the opinion that he has built a bridge from 'Is' to 'Ought', in addition to legitimizing the *raison d'être* of sociology as being practically applicable.

In summary, in relation to the question of science and values, Durkheim, as opposed to Weber, sees it as being both possible and desirable for sociology to assign goals. Like Weber, he is of the opinion that there is a distinction between 'Is' and 'Ought'. As opposed to Weber, however, he holds the view that the distinction does not have the character of an insurmountable gulf. Drawing an analogy from medicine and biological thinking, Durkheim is also of the opinion that he is able to build a bridge from 'Is' to 'Ought' by distinguishing between the normal and the pathological. This enables the sociologist to evaluate the extent to which social facts are as they ought to be and, if this is not the case, then to indicate what might possibly be done with them. Hence, also with respect to the view on the possibility of dealing with values scientifically, Durkheim must be said to be more optimistic than Weber.

Whereas this chapter and the two chapters preceding it have primarily dealt with epistemological aspects of Weber's and Durkheim's methodological views, I will now shift the perspective slightly. In the next two chapters, I will examine issues tied to the question about how to explain social phenomena. However, this does not lead to any methodological engagement between Weber and Durkheim.

6
METHODOLOGICAL INDIVIDUALISM

Although Weber and Durkheim themselves did not use the terms 'methodological individualism' and 'methodological collectivism', the concepts can still be used to capture a number of their fundamental methodological positions regarding the question as to how explanations ought to be established. Here, methodological individualism is defined as the view that, in principle, the explanation of social phenomena ought to be carried out in terms of individuals' objectives, characteristics, behaviour, attitudes or the like. In other words, explanation of social phenomena should ultimately be reduced to the individual level. Methodological collectivism can then be established as a denial of this principle. The two terms, methodological individualism and methodological collectivism, thus form a dichotomy, even though the positions of various theoreticians cannot in practice always be placed in a straightforward manner in relation to this dichotomy.

In relation to the subject–object issue, it was earlier made clear that, whereas Durkheim focuses on social facts (cf. the section in Chapter 4 on Durkheim: inductivism), Weber wants to make meaningful social action the core object of sociology (cf. the section in Chapter 4 on Weber: neo-Kantianism). With such views on what constitutes the object of sociology, it is to be expected that Durkheim places himself within a form of methodological collectivism, whereas Weber represents a form of methodological individualism.

Weber: methodological individualism

In his late methodological writings, Weber defines sociology and its object in the following terms:

> *Sociology*, a word often used in quite diverse ways, *shall mean here: a science which seeks interpretative understanding* (deutend verstehen) *of social action, and thereby will causally explain its course and effects.* By 'action' is meant human behaviour linked to a subjective meaning (*Sinn*) on the part of the actor or actors concerned; such behavior may be overt or occur inwardly – whether by positive action, or by refraining from such action, or by acquiescence to some situation. *Such behaviour is 'social' action where the meaning intended by actor or actors is related to the behavior of others, and conduct so oriented.*
>
> $$(BSC/GAW: 312)^{[1]}$$

Social action thus constitutes the object of sociology. In the same breath, it is also clear that Weber will explain social action both causally and on the basis of an interpretative understanding. His methodological individualism, merely hinted at here, later becomes clearer when he elaborates on his definition of how action is to be understood: 'Action, in the sense of meaningfully understandable orientation of one's own behaviour, is for us always understood as the behaviour of one or more *individual persons*' (*BSC/GAW*: 320).[2] In other words, from a sociological perspective, only individuals can act meaningfully. The object of sociology must therefore inevitably be linked to individuals.

In the same context, Weber touches upon the question relating to the sociological relevance of concepts for collective bodies. In some respects, he regards collective terms such as the concept of 'state' as inevitable, including the legal dogmatic context:

> For other cognitive purposes such as in law, or for purely practical ends, it might be useful (and indeed unavoidable) to

treat social constructs (*Gebilde*) (the 'state', 'association', 'companies', 'charitable foundations') as if they were individual persons with rights and duties, or as the performers of legally relevant action. For the interpretative understanding of action by means of sociology *these constructs remain merely processes and specific behavioural relationships on the part of individual people, since for us these are the sole understandable agents* (Träger) *of meaningfully oriented action.*

(BSC/GAW: 320)[3]

Even though, strictly speaking, his use of the word '*Träger*' – also meaning 'carrier' – is parallel to Marx's conception in *Capital* of human beings as carriers (*Träger*, of class interests), which is conventionally considered a form of methodological collectivism,[4] Weber emphasizes how only individuals in collective bodies, such as states and corporations, can bear meaningfully oriented action. Collective bodies cannot act independently. Elsewhere, he also writes, again using the state concept as an example:

Finally, the aim of the approach: the '[interpretive] understanding', is the reason why interpretive sociology (in our sense) treats the single individual and his action as its most basic unit, its 'atom' (if we for once allow ourselves this, in itself questionable, analogy). . . . For sociology, concepts such as 'state', 'co-operative association', 'feudalism' and similar ones designate (generally speaking) categories of certain kinds of joint human action; and *it is therefore the task of sociology to reduce them to action that can be 'understood', which without exception means: the action of the participating individual human beings.*

(CMW/GAW: 280–1)[5]

In other words, one of the purposes of interpretive sociology is to reduce joint human action of phenomena, to which collective concepts such as 'state', 'association', etc. refer, to the actions of participating individuals. Even though the object of sociology – social action – is also tied to meaning that the individuals bear (*Träger*), the object of sociology is necessarily tied to individuals. Individuals alone can act

Methodological individualism 51

meaningfully. Against that background, it is hard not to conclude that, according to Weber, sociological explanations of collective bodies must in principle be carried out on, or reduced to, the individual level. Weber is thus a methodological individualist.

In his later methodological writings, however, Weber is not categorically against arguments implying methodological collectivism, although he draws narrow limits for their scientific value. He thus discusses the scientific relevance of 'organic' sociology. Here, he appears to refer primarily to a sociology explaining societal behaviour on the basis of 'the whole' of society, analogous to explanations of the functioning of organs on the basis of their significance for 'the body' or 'the whole' (*GAW*: 554). Weber thus accepts such functionalistic ways of thinking as scientifically relevant for his interpretive sociology, for example by establishing tentative bases for further analysis. For Weber, methodological collectivism in the form of organic sociology can thus be of unquestionable relevance to the research process and can, therefore, be heuristically significant (*GAW*: 554–8). Even in the case of sociological analyses of a socialistic economy, however, the sociologist must focus on individuals and their actions. It is from this point that the real scientific, sociological work begins:

> Even a socialist economy has to be interpretatively understood 'individualistically', on the basis of the actions of individuals, the types of functionaries that emerge in it . . . For even there the most significant empirical sociological work always begins with the question: Which motives determined and do determine the *individual* functionaries and members of this 'association' to behave in such a way that the association was created and continues to exist? *All functional concept formation which begins at the level of the 'whole' is only a preliminary for such an investigation*, a preparation whose utility and indispensability – if done properly – no one can dispute.
>
> (*BSC/GAW*: 324)[6]

Thus, Weber is fully aware of the inevitability of collective concepts. However, he warns strongly against the hypostatization of such concepts and against 'false conceptual realism'. Concepts such as state, church, nation and companies have no ontological counterpart. In principle, such collective bodies can only act and be understood sociologically through the meaningful social behaviour of individuals (*GAW*: 24–5, 195, 552–4). Even though some sociological approaches implying methodological collectivism may be heuristically fruitful, and even though the use of collective concepts is inevitable, Weber's own fundamental position is in line with methodological individualism. Social relationships can – and ultimately must – be explained on the level of the individual.

Durkheim: methodological collectivism

As already mentioned, Durkheim asserts that social facts constitute the primary research object for sociology (cf. the section in Chapter 4 on Durkheim: inductivism). Moreover, they specifically constitute the exclusive subject field for sociology, as they are collective bodies and cannot be reduced to the individual level. Although the social facts might not be readily available to the senses, Durkheim reasons that we have an indirect approach to social facts, and the social facts are real, they are external in relation to the individual and they have a coercive impact on the individual (cf. the section in Chapter 3 on Durkheim: a cosmos perception, and the section in Chapter 4 on Durkheim: inductivism). The social facts are new kinds of phenomenon that do not emerge from, nor can be reduced to, the individual level, even though they are inherent to the individual:

> They constitute, thus, a new variety of phenomena; and it is to them exclusively that the term 'social' ought to be applied. And this term fits them quite well, for it is clear that, *since their source is not in the individual, their substratum can be no other than society*, either the political society as a whole or some one of the partial groups it includes, such as religious denominations, political, literary, and occupational associations, etc.
>
> (*The Rules*: 3)[7]

For Weber, collective concepts such as state, church and corporation have no ontological counterpart, whereas Durkheim, as a matter of principle, emphasizes their real existence. In support of this view, he characteristically applies a dualistic argument. The individual is juxtaposed with society, after which Durkheim, via a process of elimination, concludes that, because the social facts cannot have their origins in the individual, they must therefore come from society. The dualistic argumentation is also manifested as a tendency towards structural determinism in Durkheim. In a discussion of the individual–society relationship and collective representations, he expresses himself in rather sharp tones:

> But one would be strangely mistaken about our thought if, from the foregoing, he drew the conclusion that sociology according to us, must, or even can, make an abstraction of man and his faculties. It is clear, on the contrary, that the general characteristics of human nature participate in the work of elaboration from which social life results. But they are not the cause of it, nor do they give it its special form; they only make it possible. Collective representations, emotions, and tendencies are caused not by certain states of the consciousness of individuals but by the conditions in which the social group in its totality is placed. Such actions can, of course, materialize only if the individual natures are not resistant to them; *but these individual natures are merely the indeterminate material that the social factor molds and transforms.*
>
> (*The Rules*: 106)[8]

Here, structural determinism manifests itself in connection with the juxtaposition of individual and society inasmuch as the individual becomes the weak link. His/her consciousness is simply squashed under the pressure of the structure of society. However, this tendency is not unambiguous in Durkheim.

In addition to the individual–society juxtaposition, a holistic argumentation is another one of Durkheim's arguments for how the social facts constitute an independent, objectively existing research object. The characteristics of the whole are different from those of the parts, and the whole has primacy over the parts:

54 Methodological individualism

> The objection may be raised that a phenomenon is collective only if it is common to all members of society, or at least to most of them – in other words, if it is truly general. This may be true; but it is general because it is collective (that is, more or less obligatory), and certainly not collective because general. It is a group condition repeated in the individual because imposed on him. *It is to be found in each part because it exists in the whole, rather than in the whole because it exists in the parts.*
>
> (*The Rules*: 9)[9]

Society is an independent entity, separate from its parts and from the sum of individuals. The individuals – or rather, the individual – constitute the weak link in relation to the society. Social facts are real and constitute the object of sociology. Against the background of these positions, Durkheim predictably avoids explaining social facts on the basis of individuals. As he writes in his annotated table of contents in *The Rules*: 'The social facts can *only* be explained by social facts'.[10] Durkheim not only holds this view, but also believes that he has demonstrated that this is indeed the only possibility for explaining a social fact: '*We have shown* that a social fact can be explained *only* by another social fact' (*The Rules*: 145).[11] Thus, Durkheim is a methodological collectivist. For him, it would be the end of sociology as an independent science if social facts could be reduced in principle to the individual level and be accounted for on the basis of scientific disciplines that, like the psychology of his day, have the individual or his/her consciousness as its object of analysis.

In summary, then, Durkheim's argumentation for the objective existence of social facts is virtually found to raise the conceptual realism that Weber warns against to a scientific norm. Durkheim rejects the explanation of social facts on the individual level, whereas Weber, on the basis of the meaning of the action, will explain social action on the individual level. Weber and Durkheim thus represent methodological individualism and methodological collectivism, respectively.

Finally, when considering the extent to which they are open to each other's point of view, Weber must be said to be heuristically open to an organic sociology, although without recognizing its explanatory value. Conversely, Durkheim must be regarded as being more dismissive of sociological views à la Weber that entail the explanation of social facts and social life on the individual level: 'The determining cause of a social fact should be sought among the social facts preceding it and *not among the states of the individual consciousness*' (*The Rules*: 110).[12] This formulation is not merely in harmony with Durkheim's methodological collectivism; at the same time, it hints at a type of explanation that the sociologist can and ought to make use of when explaining social facts: causal explanations. In principle, this is a question about which types of explanation Weber and Durkheim hold to be valid. This question will therefore be addressed in the next chapter.

7

TYPES OF EXPLANATION

The previous chapter accounted for how Durkheim and Weber have different views on the extent to which sociological explanations of social relations can and ought to be reduced to the individual level. This chapter looks more closely at which types of explanation Durkheim and Weber regard as being valid. Here, three types of explanation are relevant: intentional, functional and causal. Here again, Weber and Durkheim have different views, although they also somewhat overlap. Their views genuinely become apparent when we consider how they determine the content of the object of sociology in greater detail. I therefore begin with their respective characterizations of sociology and its object, before dealing with the three types of explanation, one at a time.

Durkheim: functional and causal explanations

In the preface to the second edition of *The Rules*, Durkheim provides a very concise definition of sociology in a discussion of the characteristics of social facts. Durkheim says that social facts are created by a plurality of individuals outside each individual and institute certain ways of acting and certain judgements, which can be referred to as 'institutions':

One can, indeed, without distorting the meaning of this expression, designate as 'institutions' all the beliefs and all the modes of conduct instituted by the collectivity. *Sociology can then be defined as the science of institutions, of their genesis and of their functioning.*

(*The Rules*: lvi)[1]

Durkheim's definition of sociology indirectly indicates which types of explanation sociology ought to draw upon when explaining social facts. Sociology ought to be able to explain how social facts function, that is, use functional explanations, and it ought to be able to account for their genesis; for Durkheim, this means making use of causal explanations.

First, as regards functional explanations, in the light of Durkheim's methodological collectivism and the inspiration he draws from biological and organism-oriented thinking, his interest in utilizing functional explanations is hardly surprising; such explanations are also found in biology.

However, Durkheim is somewhat unclear when it comes to what he specifically means in terms of the function of a social fact. He indicates that he understands function as a social end, as opposed to the useful results that a social fact may create: 'The function of a social fact ought always to be sought in its relation to some social end' (*The Rules*: 110–11).[2] At the same time, however, Durkheim also says that function is about useful effects or utility. Moreover, it is said that it is about investigating whether there is correspondence between the social fact and the general needs of the social organism in question (*LRLMS*: 95, 109, 118, 124). The latter sense brings Durkheim closer to what Weber refers to as an 'organic' sociological approach (cf. the section in Chapter 6 on Weber: methodological individualism). Here, the function is that which is necessary, or at least important, for maintaining the whole of a social entity or an organism. At the same time, in connection with discussions on how to go about explaining social facts, Durkheim is quite aware of the limitations of the validity of functional explanations. He thus criticizes sociologists who believe that the function of a phenomenon can account for its emergence (*LRLMS*: 90). However, this is neither the case in sociology nor biology:

58 Types of explanation

> It is, moreover, a proposition true in sociology, as in biology, that the organ is independent of the function – in other words, while remaining the same, it can serve different ends. *The causes of its existence are, then, independent of the ends it serves.*
>
> (*The Rules*: 91)[3]

Neither biology nor sociology necessarily includes any connection between organ and function. The emergence or genesis of a social fact cannot be explained by its function. Thus, two types of explanation therefore become necessary in order to be able to provide valid sociological explanations. Durkheim articulates this view in the following maxim or rule: 'When, then, the explanation of a social phenomenon is undertaken, we must seek separately *the efficient cause which produces it and the function it fulfils*' (*The Rules*: 95).[4] In other words, it is necessary to use both causal and functional explanations (*LRLMS*: XV, XXII, 95, 96). In addition, Durkheim gives causal explanations the heuristic primacy in the sense that it is better to begin by looking for the cause than for the function of a social fact (*LRLMS*: 96, 147).

Second, as regards causal explanations, Durkheim builds on the fundamental assumption that the principle of causality also applies to sociology. He articulates the principle of causality in the following way: 'A given effect has *always* a *single* corresponding cause' (*The Rules*: 128).[5] When using causal explanations, science must presuppose the validity of the principle of causality. Durkheim makes the argument – probably directed at Hume – that philosophers are alone in having challenged this principle (*LRLMS*: 126). In connection with the considerations regarding how sociology can methodologically prove the existence of causal relationships between social facts, Durkheim bases his reasoning on one of Mill's methods, that is, the method of concomitant variations. In arguing for the explanatory potential of this method, Durkheim uses suicide and education as examples:

> For example, we can establish in the most certain way that the tendency to suicide varies directly with education. But it is impossible to understand how erudition can lead to suicide; such an explanation is in contradiction to the laws of psychology. Education, especially the elementary branches of knowledge,

Types of explanation   59

reaches only the more superficial regions of consciousness; the instinct of self-preservation is, on the contrary, one of our fundamental tendencies. It could not, then, be appreciably affected by a phenomenon as far removed and of so feeble an influence. *Thus we come to ask if both facts are not the consequence of an identical condition.* This common cause is the weakening of religious traditionalism, which reinforces both the need for knowledge and the tendency toward suicide.

(*The Rules*: 132)[6]

Durkheim's view on the principle of causality fits together with his positive perceptions on induction and the necessity of using causal explanations. He attempts to explain the connection between education and suicide in causal terms, referring to causes and distances between zones of consciousness, and identifies the erosion of religious traditionalism as the common cause with respect to the relationship between education and suicide.

Third, when it comes to explanations of social facts pointing in the direction of intentional explanations, Durkheim is sceptical, if not downright negative, towards individual-based intentional explanations, not just in this case, but also in principle. Considering his most radical formulations of explanation of social facts on the basis of the individual's consciousness, intentions, motives, objectives, etc., there is talk of a fairly sceptical view, if not an outright rejection. This position becomes apparent in an implicit discussion of the Hobbesian problem of order. If one is to assume – erroneously, according to Durkheim – that society is established by individuals as a system of means in order to realize certain ends, these ends can only be individual. It will, then, no longer be possible to explain society and the social facts, because one will relapse into explanations resting on the individual and the individual consciousness. It is indeed true that there is no society without individuals and no collective consciousness without individual consciousness (*LRLMS*: 97–103), but:

The group thinks, feels and acts quite differently from the way in which its members would were they isolated. If, then, we begin with the individual, we shall be able to understand *nothing* of

60   Types of explanation

> what takes place in the group. In a word, there is between psychology and sociology the same break in continuity as between biology and the physicochemical sciences. Consequently, *every time that a social phenomenon is directly explained by a psychological phenomenon, we may be sure that the explanation is false.*
>
> (*The Rules*: 104)[7]

Durkheim also formulates this view as a rule (cf. the section in Chapter 6 on Weber: methodological individualism): 'The determining cause of a social fact should be sought among the social facts preceding it and *not among the states of the individual consciousness*' (*The Rules*: 110).[8]

Weber: intentional and causal explanations

Like Durkheim, Weber also includes a brief definition of sociology. This is found in his late methodological writings (cf. the section in Chapter 6 on Weber: methodological individualism): 'Sociology, a word often used in quite diverse ways, shall mean here: a science which seeks *interpretative understanding* (deutend verstehen) *of social action, and thereby will causally explain its course and effects*' (*BSC/GAW*: 312).[9] As mentioned earlier (cf. Chapter 4), Weber does not share Durkheim's position on what constitutes the object of sociology. As is the case with Durkheim's definition, Weber's brief definition of sociology includes an indirect indication of which explanation types sociologists ought to utilize when explaining social phenomena. Like Durkheim, he is also of the opinion that sociology ought to use causal explanations. As opposed to Durkheim, he holds that sociology ought to build on intentional explanations – broadly speaking, explanations based on intended meaning, intentions, goals, ends, purposes, aims, objectives, motives, etc.

Taking Weber's definition of sociology at face value, his formulation indicates that the causal explanation almost becomes a result of the interpretative understanding. The view that understanding and causal explanation represent the two legs that sociology and the social sciences are supposed to rest on is consistent in *CMW/GAW*.

Types of explanation 61

First, considering intentional explanations, it is hardly surprising that intentional explanations become the preferred type of explanation in the light of Weber's methodological individualism. One of his main arguments for sociological explanations being made, in principle, on the individual level is, of course, that only individuals can act meaningfully. Sociology must be based on the subjective meaning of social behaviour for the actors themselves (cf. Chapter 6, the section on Weber: methodological individualism).

Weber is fully aware of how emotions and feelings can steer actions. It is by no means possible to categorize all social activity in an ends–means rationality scheme. This is entirely in keeping with ends–means rational actions together with value-rational, affectual and traditional actions being included as the four types in his typology of action. Weber draws attention to how concrete social behaviour can involve combinations of these types and is closer to, or farther away from, these four types, which are attributed ideal type status (*GAW*: 565–7). The instrumental or ends–means rationality is presumably to be regarded as the methodologically most fundamental type of action. Thus, Weber claims in both his early and late methodological writings that this type of action is the easiest to understand off-hand:

> Any conscious reflection on *the most fundamental elements of meaningful human action is from the beginning tied to the categories 'ends' and 'means'.*
>
> (*CMW/GAW*: 102)[10]

> That 'kind of' meaning-related structure of *action that is most immediately accessible to 'understanding'* is action that is, subjectively, strictly rationally oriented towards *means* (subjectively) deemed to be unambiguously adequate for attaining (subjectively) unambiguous and clearly comprehended *ends*.
>
> (*CMW/GAW*: 276)[11]

By explaining social actions on the basis of the agent's ends, the sociologist must typically attribute some degree of rationality to the agent. One of Weber's main theses is that capitalism, bureaucracy and science have been among the factors contributing to the growth of

62 Types of explanation

the instrumentally rational way of thinking and acting since the Reformation, and that this rationalization process has supplanted world views and ways of thinking attributing magic to the world and resulting in loss of magic (*GAW*: 593–4). However, this does not lead Weber to claim that people generally act rationally.

For example, a stockbroker's behaviour, which obviously is typically steered by an objective regarding the achievement of financial gain, can be irrational in connection with a stock market panic. Nevertheless, such behaviour would be meaningful and accessible for an intentional explanation (*GAW*: 227, 432, 435–6, 534, 544–5, 548).

Even though social activity is basically understandable in principle, Weber is also aware of the fact that it can be difficult, in practice, for the sociologist and historian to cast light on, and know the motives behind, concrete social behaviour (*GAW*: 279–82, 561–2).

Further along these lines, Weber also appears to be of the opinion that an attempt at understanding an action and the motive behind it has the character of a hypothesis and that it must be accompanied by empirical verification, which typically builds upon causal explanation (*GAW*: 129–30, 428, 548). Supplementing intentional explanation with causal explanation presumably demands that Weber believes that the explanation of action on the basis of meaning, purposes, goals or motives cannot proceed in a causal manner; otherwise, it is difficult to see why he should regard causal explanation as being insufficient. Nevertheless, he would occasionally appear to be close to claiming that goals are also of a causal nature:

> A 'goal' is, as we see it, *the idea of a result that becomes the cause of an action*; and we shall take it into account, *as we take into account any cause* that contributes or may contribute to a significant result.
> (*CMW/GAW*: 120–1)[12]

Such wording seems slightly problematic on the grounds that it appears to weaken Weber's insistence on the necessity of applying both intentional and causal explanations. And the fact that he operates with 'explanatory understanding' – that is, without opposing explanation and understanding – does not make things easier, although he is not necessarily inconsistent.

The latter relationship thus becomes apparent in how Weber distinguishes between direct and explanatory understanding. The direct understanding of an action, for example a woodcutter cutting wood, would appear immediately or intuitively understandable in Weber. Conversely, the explanatory understanding goes a step deeper by requiring that the behaviour be couched in a context of meaning, which also indicates a motive behind the action. For example, the woodcutter is possibly working for a wage and thus displaying this behaviour in order to earn money (*GAW*: 546–7). Weber thus indicates that explanatory understanding requires consideration of motives. In the same context, he would also appear to define how he understands explanation: 'For a science concerned with the meaning of action, "explanation" amounts to: *identification of the meaning context to which a directly understandable action belongs, corresponding to its subjectively intended meaning*' (*BSC/GAW*: 316).[13] This indirectly indicates how Weber, in order to explain action, requires that it is directly understandable and must be couched in a context of meaning, and that the point of departure is the subjective meaning that the action has for the acting individual.

The way Weber begins with the subjective meaning of the acting individual when examining social action and the requirement regarding the use of intentional explanations as necessary for establishing a valid explanation has an important consequence. In concrete analyses, he becomes methodologically obligated to take the individuals' consciousness and world views, or '*Weltanschauung*', together with the objectives and motives that their actions seek to realize at face value, at least as long as his data suggest that the individuals really have these motives or this world view. This applies, regardless of whether Weber himself shares the same values or not. Weber is conscious of this methodological consequence (*GAW*: 433, 535–6). At this point, he can be seen as standing in contrast to Durkheim's scepticism towards intentional explanations and attempts at explaining social phenomena on the basis of individual consciousness (cf. the section on Durkheim: functional and causal explanations, on p. 56). For Weber, however, intentional explanations are necessary but not sufficient. He maintains that valid explanations must build upon both understanding and causal analysis.

64 Types of explanation

Second, as regards causal explanation and the relationship to intentional explanations, Weber explicitly rejects that these two types of explanation exclude one another. On the contrary, he claims that they complement one another:

> However, sociology would protest against the assumption that [interpretive] 'understanding' and causal 'explanation' have *no* relationship with another. It is true that they begin their work at opposite poles of what happens. In particular, *the statistical frequency of a certain behaviour does not make it one jot more 'intelligible' in terms of its meaning; and, in itself, a maximum of 'intelligibility' [of an occurrence] in no way speaks in favour of its frequency* – indeed, in the case of absolute subjective purposive rationality, it will mostly speak against it.
>
> (*CMW/GAW*: 279)[14]

Even though Weber consistently maintains the complementarity between the two types of explanation, he seems less consistent when it comes to a more precise accounting of how they are to be combined. Among multiple possibilities, he would appear to indicate at least two different ways of combining the two types. In both cases, ideal-typical considerations play an implicit or explicit role. In his late methodological writings, Weber couples understanding together with rules for behaviour and statistics-based observations, as in the quote above regarding the relationship between understanding and statistical frequency. In his early writings, he focuses more on forms of analysis building upon what he later also refers to as a 'thought experiment' (*GAW*: 549), or what can also be described as counterfactual analysis.

In his early methodological writings, Weber thus points out how the sociologist, or rather the historian, must apply their interest-conditioned perspective to select the individual phenomena that they wish to understand from the chaotic and unique multiplicity of phenomena. The conditions for their emergence and their effects can and should then be analysed causally. This entails an assessment of the connection between two individual phenomena by hypothetically eliminating the first in order to apply ordinary causal rules of experience to assess whether this will have an impact on the other phenomenon

Types of explanation 65

and its subsequent emergence. Weber describes this procedure in the following way:

> But the real question [that we are faced with] is of course the following: What are the logical operations by means of which we can acquire the insight – and underpin it by demonstration – *that* such a causal relationship exists between those 'important' elements of the outcome and certain components among the infinity of determining factors? Obviously, [we can]not [do so] simply by 'observing' the sequence of events . . . *the causal imputation is carried out in the form of an intellectual process that comprises a number of abstractions. The first and decisive one is the following: We imagine that one or a few of the actual causal components of the sequence [of events] are modified in a certain direction and ask ourselves whether, if the conditions of the sequence of events have been thus modified, the outcome would be the same* (as far as the 'important' points are concerned) or what other outcome 'could have been expected'.
>
> (*CMW/GAW*: 173–4)[15]

This kind of intellectual process and causal imputation corresponds to counterfactual analysis. Here, one is, in principle, explaining a phenomenon, typically the emergence of an event, by referring to a previously occurring phenomenon that is seen as a necessary condition for the emergence of the event. The causal connection is established in its pure form by assessing whether the event (the effect) would have come about if the first phenomenon (the condition/cause) had not appeared. If the assessment is negative, that is, that the event would not have occurred without the occurrence of the first phenomenon, the first phenomenon is then, by using a counterfactual claim, considered a necessary condition for the subsequent event. Weber describes the core in such a 'thought experiment': 'In order to grasp the real causal interconnections, we construct unreal ones' (*CMW/GAW*: 182).[16]

In his later writings, Weber shifts the perspective on the compatibility of intentional and causal explanations. In keeping with the move away from the historical and towards the sociological, he

66 Types of explanation

increasingly draws upon regular behaviour and statistical considerations such as relative frequencies. As part of an example of calculation, he distinguishes between meaningfully adequate and causally adequate behaviour. Meaningfully adequate behaviour is typically characterized by a context of meaning. For example, we can observe how a person or group of persons has understood the rules for addition and thereafter typically adds up correctly. Causally adequate behaviour is tied to the probability that, on the basis of our experience, a sequence of events will occur or repeat themselves; that is, the probability that the person or persons will arrive at the correct result. Weber elaborates on this distinction from an explanatory perspective:

> *Causal explanation* therefore involves the idea that some degree of probability exists – ideally (although rarely) exactly quantifiable – that one particular observed (internal or external) event will be succeeded by another particular event (or will occur at the same time).
>
> *Correct causal interpretation* of a concrete action requires its apparent course and motive to be accurately recognized and meaningfully understood in context. A correct causal interpretation of a typical action (those actions open to understanding) requires that the origin typically claimed for such action appears to a degree both meaningfully adequate, and that this origin can to some extent also be described as causally adequate. *In the absence of such meaningful adequacy we have only an incomprehensible (or incompletely understandable) statistical probability, even where there is a very significant, precisely quantifiable probability of a regular event occurring (whether overt or psychic). By contrast, even the most unambiguous meaningful adequacy has significance for sociological knowledge only to the extent that a correct causal statement, as proof of the existence of a (somehow specifiable) likelihood that the action in fact tends to take an apparently meaningful course with specifiable frequency, or something close to it (either on average, or in a 'pure' case), can be instanced.* Only those statistical regularities which correspond to the understandably intended meaning of a social action are in the sense used here understandable types of action, i.e. 'sociological rules'.
>
> (*BSC/GAW*: 319)[17]

Types of explanation   67

In addition to Weber here repeating the necessity and adequacy of establishing valid explanations via causal and intentional explanations, it is worth noting how he points out that even the most precise statistical correlations would be unintelligible in the absence of the element of meaning. This view is worth elaborating on in light of Durkheim's previously mentioned attempt at explaining the connection between education and suicide in causal terms (cf. the section on Durkheim: functional and causal explanations, on p. 56).

Durkheim claims that it is possible to conclude with great certainty that the tendency towards suicide varies according to the tendency towards education, but that it is impossible to understand how education can lead to suicide. From an explanatory perspective, Weber would probably agree with Durkheim that it would be fine to have statistical data on the correlations between education and suicide. They would presumably also agree on the causal direction between the two variables, as suicide rarely leads to education! Moreover, Weber would presumably also agree with Durkheim's statement that it is impossible to understand how education in itself can lead to suicide. And, further, he might also agree that the explanation is to be found in the withering of religious traditionalism, which, according to Durkheim, simultaneously reinforces the need for knowledge and the propensity to suicide. But this is where their agreement would end if they were both to remain true to their respective methodological positions. For Weber, the context would become unintelligible if it were not possible to establish a meaningful connection between education and suicide with reference to the withering of religious traditionalism, or possibly a different factor. And Durkheim could hardly be expected to go along with that. On principle, Durkheim refuses to use intentional explanations and would instead explain the concrete relationship in causal terms of distance and the potential impacts between zones of consciousness and the like. At best, Durkheim would supplement causal explanations of social relationships with functional explanations.

Third, and finally, as far as Weber's view on functional explanations is concerned, it is found that, whereas Durkheim dismisses both intentional explanations (cf. the section on Durkheim: functional and causal explanations, on p. 56) and methodological individualism

68 Types of explanation

(cf. the section in Chapter 6 on Durkheim: methodological collectivism, on p. 52), Weber must be regarded as being more open to functional explanations. Weber has already been revealed (cf. the section on Weber: methodological individualism, in Chapter 6) to be open on the heuristic level to an 'organic' sociology that will explain social activity on the basis of its importance for 'the whole', analogous to the biological explanation of the function or the activity of an organ for the body. However, he does not consider functional explanations as being valid in the context of sociology.

In summary, then, it can be said that, as regards the question about types of explanation, Durkheim and Weber both favour causal explanations as the one valid type of explanation. Weber will supplement causal explanations with intentional explanations, whereas Durkheim will use functional explanations. Moreover, Weber would appear to be more open to Durkheim's functional explanations than Durkheim is to Weber's intentional explanations.

Having dealt with the explanatory dimension in this and the previous chapter, the last two substantive chapters are devoted to Durkheim's and Weber's views on concept formation and laws. Once again, the differences prove more conspicuous than the similarities.

8

FORMATION OF CONCEPTS

This chapter examines the views held by Weber and Durkheim on which types of concept are most scientifically relevant and how they are formed. As becomes apparent, Durkheim prefers generic concepts. Conversely, Weber is renowned for his use of ideal types, although he does not insist on this term (*GAW*: 535), also speaking in Kantian terms about 'pure types'. As far as Weber is concerned, I focus mostly on the views expressed in his early methodological writings. On the one hand, shifts can be traced in his late writings on his views on the ideal type, inasmuch as he explicitly refers to sociology as a discipline, no longer only referring to history or the cultural sciences. On the other hand, he sticks to some of his former perceptions and refers to his previous points of view in 'The "Objectivity" of knowledge in social sciences and social policy' of the purpose of the ideal type (*GAW*: 548, 562).

Weber: ideal types

As to how ideal types are formed, Weber, beginning with the notion of the market in economic theory, characterizes the ideal type as a construct that, on the basis of a one-sided perspective, is achieved by a theoretical accentuation of certain aspects of reality (*GAW*: 191).

70 Formation of concepts

He elaborates slightly on this with reference to the notion of the urban economy in the Middle Ages as another example of how an ideal type is developed:

> It is obtained by means of a one-sided accentuation of one or a number of viewpoints and through the synthesis of a great many diffuse and discrete individual phenomena (more present in one place, fewer in another, and occasionally completely absent), which are in conformity with those one-sided, accentuated viewpoints, into an internally consistent mental image.
>
> (*CMW/GAW*: 125)[1]

Along with these positive characteristics, Weber presents a number of further comments with which he characterizes the ideal type concept in negative terms. First, an ideal type is not an ideal in any moral or value-related sense. The scholar can form ideal types, just as Weber himself does with respect to the Protestant ethic, of religious phenomena. Scholars can also construct ideal types for meaning and behaviour with which they do not sympathize and for phenomena that they possibly regard as being directly immoral:

> *There are ideal types of brothels as well as of religions*; and, in the former category, we find ideal types of [establishments] that would, from the point of view of contemporary police ethics, seem to be technically 'appropriate', and of others where the exact opposite is the case.
>
> (*CMW/GAW*: 130)[2]

In other words, the ideal type is normatively neutral (*GAW*: 192, 199, 535).

Second, as regards the relationship between concept and reality, the ideal type is not 'real'. Quite the contrary, it is precisely ideal: that is, the content in an ideal type concept has no ontological counterpart (*GAW*: 194–5): 'In its conceptual purity, this mental image cannot be found empirically anywhere in reality. *It is a Utopia . . .*' (*CMW/GAW*: 125).[3] However, Weber is not entirely unambiguous on this point, as he also writes that the ideal type is seldom found in reality (*GAW*: 396).

Third, Weber stresses that it is not possible to capture necessary tendencies in historical development or actual forces in history by use of the ideal type or by any other means:

> However, it must be admitted that nothing is more dangerous than the legacy of naturalistic prejudice, which consists in *mixing up theory with history*. This may take various forms: it may be believed that those conceptual images contain the 'real' substance or the 'essence' of historical reality; or the concepts may be used as a Procrustean bed into which history is to be forced; or the 'ideas' may even be hypostatized as a 'true' reality that exists beyond the fleeting phenomena, as real 'forces' that work themselves out in history.
>
> (*CMW/GAW*: 127)[4]

Moreover, Weber also details how the ideal type can serve at least four different research-related purposes. One of his justifications for using ideal types is that the ideal type, with its one-sided accentuation of selected aspects of the complicated reality, simplifies complicated contexts and thereby creates clarity (*GAW*: 196, 560, 562). Further, he argues that the ideal type has considerable heuristic value, as it can guide the formation of hypotheses (*GAW*: 130–1, 190, 329–30, 357–8, 548). Additionally, the ideal type is, not least, useful as an instrument for use in the comparison of different parts of empirical reality in order to investigate the extent to which they deviate from the ideal type in question (*GAW*: 130, 191, 194, 201, 535–6). As such, Weber writes:

> All descriptions of the 'essence' of Christianity, for instance, are ideal types. If they claim to be a historical representation of what can be found empirically, their validity will always and by necessity [only] be very relative and problematical; but *if, on the contrary, they are simply used as conceptual tools with which reality can be compared and against which it can be measured, they possess great heuristic value for research and high systematic value for exposition.*[5]
>
> (*CMW/GAW*: 129)

Finally, Weber also points out the significance of the ideal type in connection with providing explanations. He does not use the term 'ideal-typical explanations', speaking rather about rational constructions,

72 Formation of concepts

which we would probably refer to today as rational reconstructions. Using a recurring example, he implicitly describes how rational constructions are made:

> For instance, if we are to 'understand' the conduct of a war, we must necessarily – even if this is not done explicitly or in detailed form – imagine an ideal commander-in-chief, on each side, with [full] knowledge and constant awareness of the total situation and the distribution of the military resources on both sides, and of all the possibilities that this afforded of achieving the goal (which would be precisely defined in the concrete case) of destroying the military power of the adversary, and whose action on this basis would have been free from all mistakes or logical 'errors'. Only then will it be possible to establish precisely how the fact that the actual commanders-in-chief did *not* possess that knowledge, and *did make mistakes* – that they were, in fact, far removed from being purely rational thinking machines – causally influenced the [actual] course of events. In other words: *the rational construction is valuable here because it functions as an instrument of correct causal 'imputation'.*
>
> (*CMW/GAW*: 330)[6]

Here and elsewhere (*GAW*: 130–2, 203–4, 561), the ideal type, or the rational construction, actually works as a step in the establishment of an explanation alongside what was earlier described (cf. the Chapter 7 section on Weber: intentional and causal explanations) as counterfactual analysis in connection with causal explanation. The resulting course of events if the actors had full information and actually acted in a completely instrumentally rational manner is compared with the actual course of events and the actual result. The fact that one or more of the conditions of the rational construction have typically not been fulfilled in the actual course of events thus contributes to explaining the actual course of events. For example, the two military leaders may not have acted in an entirely instrumentally rational manner. The absence of full instrumental rationality, which otherwise could have appeared as an objective possibility for one or both of the military leaders, is attributed explanatory value in the form of effects,

Formation of concepts 73

which Weber presumably regards as being causal, on the result of the actual course of events. So again here, Weber pairs the intentional and causal explanations by allowing the rational construction to be built on actor rationality – that is, an intentional element – and simultaneously being of the opinion that the lack of fulfilment of one condition or another opens up for a causal explanation.

It must be pointed out that Weber's views on the ideal type are not necessarily entirely consistent. Weber appears to operate with different kinds of ideal type, and, whereas his late methodological writings open the sociological door wider for other types of concept formation (*GAW*: 559–62), the early methodological writings hold the view that the ideal type is a special gift to the cultural sciences (*GAW*: 189–90): 'This is because *the aim of ideal-typical concept formation is always to bring out clearly what is distinctive*, and *not* what is generic, in cultural phenomena' (*CMW/GAW*: 131).[7] Besides advancing yet another of the many purposes served by the ideal type, this view also means that concept formation in general terms such as *genus proximum et differentia specifica* has limited relevance. In his characterization of the significance of the ideal type for the description of historical phenomena, Weber writes: 'A "definition" of those syntheses of historical thought [made by historians, HJ] after the pattern "genus proximum, differentia specifica" is of course an absurdity, as any attempt [to carry it through] will show' (*CMW/GAW*: 126).[8] In Weber's early writings, the ideal type is thus the preferred conceptual tool, while what Weber labels ordinary generic concepts, that is, concepts comprising what is common to empirical phenomena (*GAW*: 202), are secondary.

Durkheim: generic concepts

Durkheim's view on how sociology ought to form scientific concepts can be presented in relation to Weber's views on the utility of the ideal type and the lack of utility of the *genus proximum* concept in relation to the cultural sciences. Durkheim is sceptical towards everyday language and is of the opinion that it is not normally precise enough for scientific purposes. Science has to develop its own definitions and not use everyday language in an unreflected manner. The justification for doing so includes how:

74 Formation of concepts

> *Every scientific investigation is directed toward a limited class of phenomena, included in the same definition.* The first step of the sociologist, then, ought to be to define the things he treats, in order that his subject matter may be known. This is the first and most indispensable condition of all proofs and verifications. A theory, indeed, can be checked only if we know how to recognize the facts of which it is intended to give an account.
>
> (*The Rules*: 34)[9]

In keeping with this justification, Durkheim, on the one hand, discusses the opportunities for capturing the inherent characteristics – or the nature – of things via definitions. On the other, he also sees problems related to such practice if it is carried out at a very early stage in an investigation. Against that background, Durkheim presents the rule that: 'The subject matter of *every sociological study should comprise a group of phenomena defined in advance by certain common external characteristics*, and all phenomena so defined should be included within this group' (*The Rules*: 35).[10] If one chooses to follow this rule, Durkheim asserts that it will then be possible to gain a footing in reality from the very first step. The manner in which the phenomena are classified will then no longer depend on the sociologist, but rather on the very nature of the things themselves (*LRLMS*: 36). According to Durkheim, the rule for how definitions must be developed by including external or empirical criteria also ensures objectivity, as the phenomena subsequently practically classify themselves.

Finally, Durkheim also formulates the requirement of the sociologist that: 'The external characteristics in terms of which he defines the objects of his researches should be as objective as possible' (*The Rules*: 44).[11] The sociologist has ample opportunities to ensure this objectivity by examining the constant features of social life and avoiding focusing on the individual manifestations of the social facts. As earlier described (cf. the Chapter 3 section on Weber: a chaos perception), Durkheim outlines how social facts are unique in that they can be crystallized, for instance in figures of speech and legal rules, without losing their identity. In this manner, the sociologist can observe social facts without subjective influences. Durkheim thus claims that: 'A legal regulation is what it is, and there are no two ways of looking at it' (*The Rules*: 45).[12]

Durkheim's views on how sociological concepts ought to be formed can thus be summarized such that sociological concepts ought to build on general definitions that divide social phenomena into classes. The definition should cover a class of social phenomenon and include empirical criteria that are recognizable in all of the elements of the class in order to capture the common external characteristics of the phenomena. They should preferably be objective in the sense that the external characteristics are constant. In general, Durkheim's view on the formation of concepts squares with Weber's perception of ordinary generic concepts as comprising what is common to empirical phenomena.

Here, in summary, it is possible to contrast the views on concept formation in Durkheim, who prefers generic concepts suited for classifying social phenomena and generalizing about social phenomena, with the corresponding views in Weber, who primarily applies ideal type concepts and emphasizes unique phenomena as scientifically relevant in his early methodological writings. Weber's and Durkheim's respective views on concept formation can be seen in the context of their views on laws. I will, therefore, examine these in the next chapter.

9
LAWS

The difference between the views in Durkheim and Weber on sociological concept formation is closely related to their respective views on laws, which can therefore be dealt with a little more succinctly. The main difference lies in how Durkheim sees the purpose of sociology as finding and establishing laws. Conversely, Weber, albeit most markedly in his early methodological writings, considers laws a means for research, in particular for the production of causal explanations. In connection with the views of the two men on laws, it is natural to touch briefly upon an issue related to laws and the social sciences: the question of the existence of laws necessarily steering the development of society as a whole.

Durkheim: laws as an end

Durkheim holds as a basic assumption that the principle of causality can be applied to social facts (cf. the Chapter 7 section on Durkheim: functional and causal explanations). He appears to understand the causality principle as (cf. the same section): 'A given effect has always a single corresponding cause' (*The Rules*: 128).[1] In addition, he indirectly indicates further how the principle of causality also forms the basis for the principle concerning the proportionality between cause and effect (*LRLMS*: 126–7). In other words, the more the cause is present, the more the effect will also be present.

In his discussion of the causality principle, Durkheim also touches upon a number of philosophical aspects of its validity. Presumably with Mill and Hume in mind, he thus writes: 'However, only philosophers have ever questioned the logic of the causal relation. For the scientist there is no question about it; it is assumed by the very method of science' (*The Rules*: 126).[2] And Durkheim comes close to attempting to justify the validity of the causality principle with reference to how it has thus far proven to be empirically tenable:

> All that it [sociology, HJ] asks is that the principle of causality be applied to social phenomena. Again, *this principle is enunciated for sociology not as a rational necessity but only as an empirical postulate, produced by legitimate induction.* Since the law of causality has been verified in the other realms of nature, and since it has progressively extended its authority from the physico-chemical world to the biological, and from the latter to the psychological, we are justified in claiming that it is equally true of the social world.
>
> (*The Rules*: 141)[3]

Durkheim's interest in the validity of the causality principle is probably to be found in the utility of the principle in sociology as the basis for how sociology can arrive at laws via induction. He is inclined to justify the causality principle inductively: as the principle of causality has proven itself empirically tenable in other sciences, then it must also be tenable within sociology. But Durkheim is not merely of the opinion that sociology, by virtue of the tenability of the causality principle, can arrive at laws via induction; it should also have this as one of its utmost goals. He criticizes other sociologists and Mill for accepting the axiom of the plurality of causes, which, for Durkheim, involves a denial of the universal validity of the principle of causality if it is interpreted in the sense that the same consequence is not always the result of the same antecedent. One of Durkheim's arguments against the axiom of the plurality of causes is thus that the use of comparative

78 Laws

and experimental reasoning in order to isolate causal relationships will be in vain: 'If we practice experimental reasoning in this spirit, we shall assemble in vain a considerable number of facts, for *we shall never be able to obtain precise laws or determinate relations of causality*' (*The Rules*: 128).[4] Implicit in this reasoning is that, via induction, it is possible to formulate laws and well-defined causal relations after collecting enough facts. According to Durkheim, this is precisely what the sociologist ought to do.

Durkheim's position is entirely in line with the aforementioned tendency towards inductivism (cf. the section on Durkheim: inductivism, in Chapter 4). It is also in harmony with a criticism he directs against some of the economists of his day for considering maxims for action as laws of nature, despite not having been found and established via induction (*LRLMS*: 26–7).

Durkheim is not entirely clear, but it would implicitly appear as though he understands laws as covariation, or that laws at least manifest themselves in covariation (*LRLMS*: 135). Thus, he indicates that the covariation found between two phenomena expresses a regular causal relationship in which the cause is always followed by an effect. The view is stated without reservation in the context of a discussion on the method of concomitant variations. In this connection, Durkheim claims that: 'As soon as one has proved that, in a certain number of cases, two phenomena vary with one another, *one is certain of being in the presence of a law*' (*The Rules*: 133).[5] The same opinion is formulated in the same context, although with somewhat greater reservation, when he writes that:

> *When two phenomena vary directly with each other, this relationship* [of constant concomitance as a law, HJ] *must be accepted even when, in certain cases, one of these phenomena should be present without the other.* For it may be either that the cause has been prevented from producing its effect by the action of some contrary cause or that it is present but in a form different from the one previously observed. No doubt, we need, as we say, to examine the facts anew; but certainly we must not abandon hastily the results of a methodically conducted demonstration.
>
> (*The Rules*: 131)[6]

The reservations that Durkheim is making here can be interpreted as reservation towards spurious relationships and *ceteris paribus* factors, of which he is also aware (*LRLMS*: 130).

However, as the most important aspect of a summary characterization of Durkheim's positions on laws, he undoubtedly sees the pursuit of laws as an objective for sociology. Covariation can further be interpreted as an expression of the presence of a law, although he does not make the terms for such an interpretation entirely clear, and laws can be coupled to the principle of causality in the sense that the same effect always corresponds to the same cause.

Finally, it is worth briefly addressing the question about the extent to which there are laws for the necessary development of society and humanity. Here, Durkheim seems to reject the existence of necessary historical laws of development. In an account of Comte's so-called 'Law of the three stages', according to which society is moving from a theological stage, through a metaphysical stage and towards a positive stage, Durkheim writes that:

> his [Comte's, HJ] famous law of the three stages of history has no relation of causality; if it is true, it is, and can be, only empirical. It is a bird's-eye view of the elapsed history of the human species. *It is entirely arbitrary to consider the third stage as the definitive state of humanity. Who knows whether another will not emerge from it in the future.*
>
> (*The Rules*: 119)[7]

Weber: laws as means

In Weber's early methodological writings, it is not an objective to arrive at laws or law-like connections. The interest of the social sciences in the reality of social and cultural life is based on its multiplicity and its unique and individual character. This point of view reduces the relevance of finding or presenting laws as an independent objective of knowledge (*GAW*: 170–2). Nevertheless, causal explanations of individual phenomena require knowledge of laws:

> Whenever one has to provide *a causal explanation of a 'cultural phenomenon'* . . . *knowledge of the laws of causation can never be the*

aim, but only the means of the investigation. That knowledge helps us and enables us to impute to their concrete causes those parts of the phenomena that are, in their individuality, culturally significant. Insofar as, and only insofar as, it renders that service, [the knowledge of laws] is valuable for acquiring knowledge about individual interconnections. And the more 'general' (that is, the more abstract) those laws are, the less they contribute to the causal imputation of individual phenomena and hence, indirectly, to the understanding of the significance of cultural occurrences.

(CMW/GAW: 118)[8]

Weber emphasizes the impossibility of causally explaining individual historical relationships without resorting to knowledge of causal regularities. If the scholar – *in casu* the historian – is in doubt as to the extent to which a phenomenon can be explained causally as the effect of a previously occurring phenomenon, this ultimately depends on the scholar's own judgement on the basis of their personal general experience and knowledge about the effects of the elements in play as to whether such an imputation of causality can be made. In Weber's opinion, these general relationships or regularities are not laws in the same sense as in the natural sciences. It is rather a matter of an 'adequate' cause-and-effect relationship that is associated with the category 'objective opportunity', although he refrains from accounting for this relationship in greater detail in this context (*GAW*: 178–9). In other words, he sees knowledge about laws or regularities as being indispensable for carrying out the research process as a part of causal explanation:

However, [within the cultural sciences] *the formulation of such regularities is not the aim, but an instrument of inquiry*; and whether it makes sense to formulate a regular causal connection, known to us from our daily experience, as a 'law', is in each individual case a question of expediency. For the exact natural sciences, 'laws' are the more important and valuable, the more *general* their validity; [but] for the purpose of gaining knowledge of historical phenomena in their concrete conditionality, the most *general* laws are as a rule the least valuable, because they are the

Laws   81

most devoid of substance: The more comprehensive the validity
– the scope – of a generic concept, the more [that concept] leads
us away from the richness of reality, since it must be as abstract
as possible – that is, contain a minimum of substance – in order
to cover what is common to as many phenomena as possible.
*Knowledge of what is general is never of value to us in the cultural sciences
for its own sake.*

(*CMW/GAW*: 118–19)[9]

It becomes clear here how Weber, in contrast to Durkheim, does
not see the establishing and formulation of laws as objectives or ends
in themselves, but the inclusion of 'laws' or regularities is a necessary
means or instrument in the search for scientific knowledge. At the same
time, this demonstrates, not merely the differences in Weber's and
Durkheim's views on the significance of laws, but also the related
differences in their views on concept formation. For Durkheim,
classical definitions, that is, generic concepts, become the central
concept formation, as they are suitable for capturing general relations.
For the same reason, they are of less value for Weber, whose ideal
types in his early methodological writings are about capturing and
analysing unique contexts.

However, it is possible to trace a shift in Weber's thinking in his
late methodological writings, in which he begins to accept and use the
term 'sociology' and refers to his own approach to the science as
'interpretive sociology'. For example, he retains his views on the science
of history that appear in the early methodological writings, while at
the same time introducing new opinions in connection with his openly
declared ambitions on behalf of sociology. The relatively long passage
below from one of his later writings on methodology is worth citing,
on the grounds that it not only touches upon the law issue but also
summarizes several of Weber's views on the themes that have been
analysed in the earlier chapters:

Sociology constructs concepts of types and *seeks general rules* in
events – this much has been repeatedly assumed in the foregoing.
This contrasts with the manner in which history is oriented to
the causal analysis and imputation of individual and cultural

82 Laws

significance to actions, constructs, and personalities. Conceptual formation in sociology takes its material largely, but not wholly, from realities of action also encountered in the historical perspective. In forming its constructs and *seeking their rules* it also considers whether, in so doing, it can be of any service to causal historical imputation in respect of important cultural phenomena. *As with any generalizing science abstractions are necessarily relatively empty of content as compared with the concrete reality of the historical. On the other hand it does provide an enhanced conceptual precision.* This enhancement in precision is achieved through the optimization of meaningful adequacy for which sociology strives. As has been recognized, such optimization has been quite completely achieved in respect of rational concepts, whether they be value-rational or instrumentally rational. But sociology also seeks to develop theoretical meaningfully adequate concepts in respect of irrational phenomena (mystic, prophetic, pneumatic, and affectual). . . . Of course, sociology also on occasion employs the idea of a statistically average type, a construct which does not require any special methodological elaboration. But when 'typical' cases are referred to here, it should ordinarily be assumed that the reference is to ideal types, whether rational or irrational, and which are for the most part constructed rationally (in respect of economic theory, always), and are always meaningfully adequate.

(*BSC/GAW*: 325–6)[10]

Human action must be explained both causally and on the basis of meaning, and not all action is rational – far from it. But instrumentally rational action, and in this instance Weber is also including value-rational action, would initially appear to have the greatest adequacy of meaning. Sociology is more or less working with the same reality as the science of history, but does so from a different perspective or point of view. Similarly, sociology works with ideal types, to which Weber also refers in his later writings as 'pure types' (*GAW*: 475, 560). However, these are more general and precise, and therefore also more empty of content. At the same time, sociology also works with other types of concept, such as the average concept. Finally, and in summary in relation to Durkheim, Weber here – while standing in contrast to Durkheim in his early methodological works in which sociological ambitions are absent – is, on the one hand, moving in his late methodological works towards Durkheim's view by stating that sociology is a generalizing science that has the search for general rules as an end, while, on the other hand, Weber is talking about 'seeking general rules' as opposed to Durkheim's 'finding laws'.

Finally, as regards the question about laws for the necessary development of society and humanity, it is possible to refer to Weber's aforementioned warnings against hypostasizing collective concepts (cf. the section on Weber: methodological individualism, in Chapter 6, and the one on Weber: ideal types, in Chapter 8) and believing that, through one's concepts, one has captured the essence of historical reality or can use them as a Procrustean bed that history can be forced to fit (*GAW*: 195). It would therefore seem reasonable to interpret these warnings as a rejection of laws for historical development. In this respect, Weber can be argued to be in line with Durkheim.

10

WEBER AND DURKHEIM: A METHODOLOGICAL COMPARISON

Based on Weber's and Durkheim's empirical research, *The Protestant Ethic* and *Suicide*, I have carried out a systematic comparison in the preceding chapters of the methodological views of the two social scientists in *CMW/GAW* and *The Rules*. In conclusion, I will primarily limit myself to responding to two questions: What are the main results of the analysis? And how do Weber's and Durkheim's methodological principles relate to their respective research practices in light of the analysis above?

Weber and Durkheim: two methodologies, two sociologies?

There is no reason to present a comprehensive summary of the results from the previous chapters. The main findings from the preceding analyses can simply, and without significant reservations, be summarized in Table 10.1. However, the table does call for a few comments.

Against the background of the results, it is natural to ask if Table 10.1 exaggerates the differences between the methodological views held by Weber and Durkheim. As regards the answer to this question, it is important to note the premises upon which the table rests. Although

TABLE 10.1 Comparison of the methodological views found in Weber and Durkheim

	Weber	*Durkheim*
'Social ontology'	'Chaos perception'	'Cosmos perception'
Societal vs. individual perspective	Individual perspective	Societal perspective
The relationship between sociology and its object; 'ontological' status of the object	Emphasis on the side of the subject; object of knowledge	Emphasis on the side of the object; real object
The core object of sociology	Social action	Social facts
Epistemological characteristics	Neo-Kantianism	Inductivism
Science and values	Gulf between 'Is' and 'Ought'	Bridge between 'Is' and 'Ought'
Explanation	Methodological individualism	Methodological collectivism
Valid types of explanation	Causal and intentional explanations	Causal and functional explanations
Formation of concepts	Ideal types	Generic concepts
Laws	Means	End

differences and oppositions dominate, Weber's and Durkheim's methodological views also overlap one another. This applies to the relevance of causal explanations. Next, one must remain aware of the fact that the results presented in the table for Weber lie closest to the views expressed in his early methodological writings. In his later works, his positions on some points shift towards Durkheim's. This is the case with Weber's thoughts on sociology, which concern seeking general rules. Moreover, it would appear that Weber – at least on the heuristic level – is more tolerant towards a sociology à la Durkheim than vice versa. Finally, it should be stressed that Table 10.1 reflects

86 Weber and Durkheim: methodological comparison

the results of *a* methodological comparison along *some* important methodological dimensions, but not all of the potentially relevant dimensions.

The answer, then, is that the table probably exaggerates the differences between Weber and Durkheim. Still, the distance between their methodological views and principles continues to appear great.[1] From this, the conclusion is that, in Weber and Durkheim already, there is not a single sociological method and a single unified sociology, but two rather different views at least on what sociology is and should be.[2]

One can then attempt to shift the focus away from Weber's and Durkheim's methodological principles and over to their research practices, hoping that the differences at this level are much less when they go about conducting concrete analyses. Doing so would lie entirely outside the framework of this book.[3] Instead, as emphasized in the introduction (cf. the section on 'How' Weber and Durkheim? in Chapter 1), I have chosen to proceed 'minimalistically' by examining how Weber and Durkheim, in the *CMW/GAW* and *The Rules*, respectively, 'say what one should do' rather than examining what they actually do themselves. I have also attempted to take their statements at face value and use quotes, in order to capture the formulations in which they appear to be the clearest.

This leads to the final question to be addressed here, namely the relationship between Weber's and Durkheim's methodological views and their research practice. By considering the extent to which Weber and Durkheim 'do as they say one should', it becomes possible to return to their research practice. That also gives me the opportunity to finish in the same place where I started.

Methodological principles and research practice in Weber and Durkheim

I began Chapter 2 by emphasizing a number of features characterizing the respective empirical research work carried out by Weber and Durkheim, *in casu The Protestant Ethic* and *Suicide*. Here, I focused on a number of aspects marking their methodological approaches in their concrete analyses, which led to, and were in harmony with, their methodological views, after which I systematically compared these views.

In conclusion, I will now take a little step in the opposite direction, that is, from methodological principles to practice. Using examples, I will question whether Weber and Durkheim completely respect their own methodological principles in their own empirical work. The purpose of doing so is first and foremost to show that it may occasionally be difficult for researchers, including Weber and Durkheim, to live up completely to abstract methodological principles. Two examples are adequate to cast light on some of the possible inconsistencies between their methodological principles and practice.

The first example concerns Weber, who has been characterized as a methodological individualist. Weber also warns against the hypostatization of collective concepts and rules out the capacity of collective bodies to act intentionally. In practice, he seems not to live fully up to his own principles in *The Protestant Ethic*:

> *Christian ascetism*, at first *fleeing* from the world into solitude, had already *ruled* the world which it had *renounced* from the monastery and *through the church*. But it had, on the whole, *left* the naturally spontaneous character of daily life in the world *untouched*. Now it *strode* into the market-place of life, *slammed* the door of the monastery behind it, and *undertook to penetrate* just that daily routine of life *with its methodicalness*, to *fashion* it into a [rational, HJ] life in the world, but neither of nor for this world. With what result we shall try to make clear in the following discussion.
>
> (*The Protestant Ethic*: 101)[4]

> The question of the motive forces in the expansion of modern capitalism is not in the first instance a question of the origin of the capital sums which were available for capitalistic uses, but, above all, of the development of *the spirit of capitalism*. Where it appears and *is able to work itself out*, it *produces* its own capital and monetary supplies as *the means to its ends*, but the reverse is not true.
>
> (*The Protestant Ethic*: 31)[5]

88 Weber and Durkheim: methodological comparison

Here, despite the fact that, according to Weber, only individuals are capable of acting as intentional subjects, the Protestant ethic and the capitalist spirit have become intentional subjects. They set goals for themselves, step into the social world and have an impact on the course of history by acting in an instrumentally rational manner and apparently using people unwittingly as instruments for their own purposes. Considering Weber's formulations here and in a couple of other places in *The Protestant Ethic* (*DPE*: 29, 45, 52, 135–6), there is talk of a sort of subject–object reversal. Ideal types or 'historical individuals' (*DPE*: 39) have become intentional subjects, while the historical individuals in the conventional sense have become objects or marionettes.

It is also possible to refer to an example from Durkheim that ties in to the explanatory dimension. Durkheim advances the methodological principle that social facts must be explained by social facts. This is to be brought about using both causal and functional explanations. Against the background of statistical studies, Durkheim attempts, in *Suicide*, to explain the unexpectedly low rate of suicide among Jews in comparison with both Protestants and Catholics (cf. the section in Chapter 2 on Durkheim: Protestants, Catholics – and suicide): 'It is a general law that religious minorities, *in order to protect themselves* against the hate to which they are exposed or merely through a sort of emulation, try to surpass in knowledge the populations surrounding them' (*Suicide*: 122).[6] Assuming that this law holds for social facts and that Durkheim is trying to explain a social fact, it is rather difficult to consider this a functional or a causal explanation. It looks far more like an intentional explanation.

As already stressed, none of the supposed methodological inconsistencies between principles and practice that have been pointed out here is an attempt to criticize the results of the analyses carried out by Weber and Durkheim. I am neither attempting to criticize their methodological principles nor claiming that they are generally methodologically inconsistent. The examples are merely intended to emphasize how, even though discussions of methodological principles can be relevant and difficult enough in themselves, it is not necessarily easier to live up to the principles when carrying out concrete empirical analyses in the social sciences. Neither Weber nor Durkheim limited himself to engaging in methodological discussions and analyses for the sake of methodology itself; rather, they were both also occupied in carrying out their own analyses of society, among which *The Protestant Ethic* and *Suicide* are two important examples.

NOTES

Abbreviations

1   *GAW* is a compilation of works from Weber's hand, and Bruun and Whimster's *CMW* is not entirely identical to the German *GAW*. *CMW* does not include a translation of '*Soziologische Grundbegriffe*' ('Basic sociological concepts'), which is usually related to Weber's *Wirtschaft und Gesellschaft* (*Economy and Society*). I have therefore had to find a different source for a translation of '*Soziologische Grundbegriffe*'. However, in order to emphasize that the methodological works that this book builds upon are the ones included in the German *GAW* (fifth edition), I have chosen to refer in English to *GAW* as *CMW/GAW* or *BSC/GAW*, depending on which of the two English translations is being used. The first and fifth German editions of *GAW* are not entirely identical. Where possible, all the quotes from the fifth edition of *GAW* (edited by Johannes Winckelmann) have therefore been compared with the first edition of *GAW* from 1922. The differences between the two editions in the quoted passages are few, small and insignificant in this context. Finally, as *GAW* is a compilation of works from Weber's hand, I have, at the end of each German quote, indicated from which part of *GAW* the quote stems, using notes in roman numerals in line with the table of contents in *GAW* (where possible, the English titles are identical to the titles in Bruun and Whimster's *CMW*):

- I = 'Roscher and Knies and the logical problems of historical economics' ('Roscher und Knies und die logischen Probleme der historischen Nationalökonomie');

Notes 91

- II = 'The "Objectivity" of knowledge in social sciences and social policy' (*'Die "Objektivität" sozialwissenschaftlicher und sozialpolitischer Erkenntnis'*);
- II = 'Critical studies in the logic of the cultural sciences' (*'Kritische Studien auf dem Gebiet der kulturwissenschaftlichen Logik'*);
- VIII = 'On some categories of interpretive sociology' (*'Über einige Kategorien der verstehenden Soziologie'*);
- X = 'The meaning of "value freedom" in the sociological and economic sciences' (*'Der Sinn der "Wertfreiheit" der soziologischen und ökonomischen Wissenschaften'*);
- XI = 'Basic sociological concepts' (*'Soziologische Grundbegriffe'*).

1 Weber and Durkheim

1 In light of how both Weber and Durkheim are regarded as the 'founding fathers' of modern sociology, it is not surprising that neither of them was educated as a sociologist. The lack of any professional exchange between the two is possibly explained to some extent by how they found themselves on different sides of the conflict between Germany and France in World War I. There are also other similarities and differences in their backgrounds, upbringings and academic careers.

Max Weber (1864–1920) was born in Erfurt, Germany, and grew up in an affluent home, with a politically active father and a religiously observant mother. In the course of his childhood, the family moved to Berlin. Weber, who studied law but also had an eye for history and philosophy, primarily studied in Berlin and Heidelberg. Having already become a professor of economics in 1894 in Freiburg and two years later in Heidelberg, Weber managed to overcome the intellectual boundaries of his day and wrote on a great variety of different issues. For example, he wrote about Roman agricultural law, trade leagues in the Middle Ages and the conditions of the rural labourers of his day in the areas around the Elbe. He also researched religion and the role and development of religions, without being particularly religious himself; to his mother's dismay, he was confirmed without displaying any particular religious commitment (Weber 1989: 61–3). Weber was also interested in politics and, at times, politically active. As already mentioned, he referred to himself, late in his career, as an economist and indicated that sociology, history, economics and political science were the subjects he found most interesting. A mental breakdown after the death of his father in 1897 led to Weber being inactive for a four-year period. This contributed to his having to give up his professorship in 1903 and living as an honorary professor. However, this was hardly a period of academic isolation for him. He was active in various forums, including the editing of a journal (*Archiv für Socialwissenschaft und Sozialpolitik*), and drew inspiration from his extensive travels. He was also in close contact with many of the leading German intellectuals of his day. It was first in 1919, one year after having served as a guest professor in Vienna, that he again received a professorship, this time in Munich. In relation to his day,

92 Notes

Weber was writing in a German milieu dominated by historicism and neo-Kantianism and in a field of overlapping conflicts about fundamental scientific problems. The conflicts regarding the fundamental scientific problems included the relationship between values and science; the '*Methodenstreit*', or the battle of method, in economics between 'historians' and 'theoreticians', as represented by, respectively, Gustav Schmoller and Carl Menger; and the relevance and validity of the methods of the natural sciences for the cultural and social sciences, where people such as the hermeneutic Wilhelm Dilthey and neo-Kantians such as Wilhelm Windelband and Heinrich Rickert wrote against such a variation of positivism on different bases (Fivelsdal 1976: VII ff.; Mitzman 1987: 3 ff.; Eliaeson 1988: 204 ff.; Weber 1989: 3 ff. (or: Chapter 2, as there are errors in the paging in this edition of the book); Parkin 1991: 13 ff.; Månsson 2000: 88 ff.; Andersen *et al.* 2003/I: 11 ff.).

Émile Durkheim grew up in a family of modest means, the son of a rabbi, in Epinal in Lorraine, in the border territory between France and Germany. In the course of his childhood, Durkheim decided against following in the footsteps of his father, grandfather and great-grandfather and becoming a rabbi. With his father's blessing, he instead applied to the *École Normale Supérieure* (ÉNS) in Paris. He was accepted on his third attempt, in 1879. In this period, he broke with Judaism. After completing his education at ÉNS in 1882, he began teaching. A year of study in Germany, in 1885–6, possibly contributed to strengthening his positive views on an organically inspired sociology. This possibly also contributed to Durkheim gaining employment in 1887 at the university in Bordeaux. Here, he wrote three of his most important works: *The Division of Labour in Society*, *The Rules* and *Suicide*. Like Weber, Durkheim maintained a solid research interest in religion, despite the absence of any strong, personal religious convictions, and he followed the political development of his time closely. Unlike Weber, he was interested early on, i.e. from the mid 1880s, in gaining recognition for the emerging field of sociology as an independent scientific discipline. He not only sought to realize this objective via his research but also through his other activities in the education and university system, to some extent at the expense of his research. It was with this objective in mind that he invested massive effort, beginning in 1896, as the co-founder and editor of a sociological journal (*l'Année Sociologique*). In that regard, he found himself engaged in academic work parallel to Weber's as the editor of a journal. The editorial work contributed to Durkheim being unable to complete a planned book on socialism. In 1902, he was employed at the Sorbonne. In 1913, four years before his death, he was presumably satisfied to be able to add the title 'sociology' to his professorship. His most significant source of inspiration was probably Auguste Comte, who was known for positivism and having had an influence on the term 'sociology'. As opposed to Weber, Durkheim came to advocate a sociology inspired by the natural sciences, and, with his sociology, contributed to a French objectivist or structural tradition (Fivelsdal 1972: VII ff.; Lundquist 1983:

Notes 93

IX ff.; Giddens 1986: 9 ff.; Lukes 1988: 39 ff.; Østerberg 1988: 173 ff.; Thompson 1990: 27 ff.; Guneriussen 2000: 69 ff.).

2 Without providing more than sporadic documentation (e.g. Parsons 1964: XI; Tiryakian 1966: 330; Giddens 1981: VII; Coser 1987: XXV; Giddens 1987: 182; Hamilton 1991: 7; Craib 1997: 1; Zeitlin 2001: 441; Hughes *et al.* 2003: 3–4; Ritzer and Goodman 2003: 5–6; Gane 2011: 1) for a subjective assessment, I believe that, for decades, most of the works in the secondary literature, including a number of textbooks in sociology, regard Weber and Durkheim, together with Marx, as being the founding fathers and most significant figures in sociology. Simmel, and to some degree Tönnies, Pareto and Mosca, are presumably their closest competitors. Eliaeson (2002: 123 ff.) goes against the stream and argues that Weber cannot be unconditionally regarded as one of the founders of modern sociology.

3 For example, the result of a vote carried out towards the end of the 1990s found that, among the sociologists in the International Sociological Association (ISA), Weber and Durkheim were both among the ten authors voted 'author of the century'. Weber was in front, while Durkheim brought up the rear. Correspondingly, Weber had two titles and Durkheim a single title among the ten books voted 'book of the century'. The results of this vote were found at: www.ucm.es/es/info/books.

As an example of Weber's continued relevance and significance, it is also worth mentioning a publication marking the 100-year anniversary of the publication of Weber's *The Protestant Ethic*. In the foreword, 1905 is mentioned as a year offering two significant scientific revolutions that changed how moderns thought about their own world, Einstein's in physics and Weber's in sociology (Lemert 2005: IX). The 100-year anniversary of Durkheim's *Suicide* was marked similarly; see Lester (1994).

4 I am hardly the first to deal with the differences between Weber and Durkheim, but this is worth mentioning, as this fact has contributed to the carrying out of this comparison between the two scholars. Without making any claim to having a comprehensive overview of the literature comparing them, it can tentatively be characterized as consisting of three groups, which at the same time demonstrates how interest in Weber and Durkheim is not new.

The first group primarily draws comparisons on the basis of substance. Examples from this group can be named that demonstrate some of the breadth and relevance of the substantial aspects of Weber and Durkheim's respective bodies of work. Sutherland (1970) represents an investigation of the perceptions of conflict found in Weber and Durkheim, which is presented as a negative comparative analysis in the sense that the conflict concept is not fully developed by Durkheim and is therefore difficult to draw upon when making comparisons, whereas it can be read better in Weber. Cartwright and Schwartz (1973) offer a statistical analysis of which of Durkheim's and Weber's positions on legal norms fit best together with the results produced by Cartwright and Schwartz's studies of legal mechanisms in the solution of conflicts between labour and capital in

94 Notes

selected areas of India. Despite a somewhat misleading title ('Neither Marx nor Durkheim . . . perhaps Weber'), Tiryakian (1975) does not produce a general, blanket rejection of Durkheim and Marx with a correspondingly conditional acceptance of Weber, but rather a heuristic-based assessment of the relevance of the three scholars for an analysis of the modern American society, where Weber emerges as the 'winner'. Müller (1992) analyses and argues in favour of that which the author refers to as the 'substantial convergence' (*sachliche Konvergenz*) (Müller 1992: 51) in Weber's and Durkheim's analyses of the significance of labour for humankind in modern society, and also includes comparative characterizations of other dimensions. Gould (1993) compares Durkheim's and Weber's analyses of solidarity and legitimacy.

A second group consists of analyses comparing Weber and Durkheim, possibly including other scholars, in methodological or methodologically relevant contexts. Examples from this second group include Taube (1966), who briefly compares Weber and Durkheim with respect to the delimitation of the object of sociology and examines the consequences that the differences in this regard have for their views on objectivity, causal explanations and laws in sociology. Gilbert (1976) compares Weber and Durkheim with respect to the value question and points out the (im)possibility of a value-neutral sociology. Kapsis (1977) carries out a more detailed analysis of Weber's and Durkheim's considerations regarding the use of comparative methods and analytical units in their analyses of religion, including *The Protestant Ethic* and *Suicide*. Bendix (1980) compares Weber's and Durkheim's respective views on sociology as a discipline, including its object, as well as their analyses of religion, and emphasizes the differences between them. Turner (1986) carries out an in-depth analysis and interpretation of the complicated question regarding causality and probability found in Weber and Durkheim, managing to go into detail without difficulty and account for their connections to Mill and Comte, as well as lesser-known philosophers and theoreticians. Giddens (1987) includes a brief comparison in terms of methodology and substantive analysis, with respect to the latter in relation to their perspectives on state and politics. Morrison (1990) compares Weber and Durkheim with respect to investigative procedures and relations to differences between French and German scientific traditions and holds the view that the demarcation runs between Durkheim's interest in honouring positivistic ideals (from the natural sciences) regarding method, whereas Weber stands for an interpretive ideal. Mohseni (1994) briefly argues that Weber and Durkheim – like Marx – must be read in terms of how they each raise questions in social analysis, and that only consideration in this regard renders it possible to carry out a synthesis of their respective perspectives. Nilsen (2003) carries out a more detailed analysis of the methodological individualism and methodological collectivism in Weber and Durkheim and attempts to bring out nuances in the portrayal of Weber and Durkheim as representatives of methodological individualism and methodological collectivism, respectively.

Notes   95

A third group consists of analyses – typically in the form of monographs, including anthologies – introducing or interpreting Durkheim and/or Weber and, typically, also other social scientists, often Marx, and presenting comparative reflections in that connection. Examples of such analyses include Aron (1968: 206–7, 253 ff.), who provides his personal presentations of Durkheim, Weber and others; Craib (1997: 58–9, 115–18, 142–5, 229–31, 256–60), who also draws on Marx and Simmel; and Giddens (1981: 190–247), who analyses Marx, Weber and Durkheim, primarily examining the substantial, as opposed to methodological, differences and similarities, and has primarily chosen to hold Marx up in relation to Weber and Durkheim but does not look very closely at the Weber–Durkheim relationship; this characterization also largely holds true with respect to Zeitlin (2001: IX, 194 ff.) and Hughes *et al.* (2003: 87 ff.).

In addition to the above, there are obviously also texts that *en passant* include comparisons between Weber and Durkheim, such as Hamilton (1991: 7–9), Tenbruck (1994: 367–8) or Gephart (2010: 34–5).

5 As regards the so-called Weber–Durkheim unawareness puzzle, see Tiryakian (1966: 330–2), who argues that the spirit of the day and closely related academic activities, including in relation to methodological questions, religion research and politics, as well as editorial activities for their respective journals, would have made it natural for them to have reviewed or referred to one another's work, but that World War I and the accompanying nationalism possibly explain the lack of references to one another. Seidmann (1977: 356) and Schroeter (1986: 195–6) show how editing and translation have significance with respect to criticism of sources when it comes to finding a position regarding the question as to the precise extent that Weber and Durkheim were familiar with one another's publications. Segre (1986–7: 151–6, 161–2) supports the claim regarding the necessity of source-critical studies for the solution of the puzzle; if not definitively, Segre at least makes it seem likely that Weber may have ignored Durkheim; however, this is probably not owing to war or nationalism, but possibly instead to epistemological disagreements and Weber's view on discursive norms in relation to German and foreign sociologists. Aron (1968: 224) and Lukes (1988: 397) contribute with a parenthetical reference and a note, respectively, with evidence of Weber's familiarity with Durkheim and Durkheim's lack of knowledge of Weber. Szakolczai (1996), who refers to another couple of references (Szakolczai 1996: 1), carries out a coupling between works, the authors' respective sources of inspiration and their respective circles of acquaintances, arguing that Weber and Durkheim – owing to differences in their respective backgrounds – reacted differently to the various currents in a partially overlapping academic universe (Szakolczai 1996: 59–63); Giddens (1987: 182) also refers to the Weber–Durkheim relationship as a puzzle, arguing further that Weber had some measure of familiarity with Durkheim and vice versa, but that neither of them inspired the other, and that the number of mutual references is therefore limited to a single modest reference by Durkheim

96 Notes

to Weber. In Roth (1989: XVIII), it is possible to see how Durkheim – by virtue of a review of a book written by Max Weber's wife, Marianne Weber – was at least familiar with the name 'Weber'. Finally, none of the indexes of names in the parts of *Max Weber Gesamtausgabe* published so far and being at my disposal indicates any relation from Weber to Durkheim.

6 Gane (2011), an in-depth work on *The Rules*, reveals how the assumption of regarding *Suicide* as the quintessential use of *The Rules* is not tenable (Gane 2011: 50).

7 Wagner and Zipprian (1994: 9–24) present an occasionally critical discussion of the extent to which it is possible meaningfully to refer to a single *'Wissenschaftslehre'* in Weber, which of his works have been included in the various editions of the posthumously published *GAW* and in more or less alternative publications, which of his works – after a content-related assessment – can be included under such a heading, and the extent to which there is talk of a cohesive perception in Weber's methodology or breaks in this regard. Münch (2004) represents an attempt to carry out the non-existent dialogue between Weber and Durkheim.

8 As regards Weber's somewhat concealed polemics, Jacobsen (1991: 3, 114) presents concrete examples, in this case in relation to Rickert. Jacobsen also warns that Weber is a 'footnote tactician' and that one should avoid taking Weber's references completely at face value. With respect to Weber's writing style, obviously the readers who may have needed to give up along the way have not chosen to write about him. Nevertheless, as a matter of curiosity, at least one reader of Weber, although not having given up, is of the opinion that the reward gained from reading him is not worth the effort required to read him. Andersson thus quotes German historian Golo Mann for assessing Weber's 'legalese' writing style as having given occasion to the 'most wonderful sentence constructions' (Andersson 1977: 211). Andersson himself delivers the following salvo to Weber in passing:

> He who reads Max Weber's work must ask himself the question: Why does the man write in such terribly woody and murky terms [Swedish: *fruktansvärt träaktigt och grötigt*]? It is to say the least painful to read him, and some of his writings are simply impossible to read in any reasonable sense of the word.
>
> (Andersson 1977: 26)

9 The quotes from Weber and Durkheim have been taken from English translations. In that sense, there is not talk of Weber's and Durkheim's own formulations. And translation can be contested. That goes for both Durkheim and Weber (see, for instance, Gane (2011: 2) and Hillmann (2002), respectively). As already mentioned, however, the corresponding parallel quotes from the German and French originals are presented in the notes.

10 Merely some loose arguments to render probable the claim about the development in the overwhelming amount of literature on Durkheim and,

not least, Weber. In the preface to the republication of a renowned Durkheim biography, Steven Lukes noted, in the mid 1980s, more than a decade after the publication of the first edition (1973), that some six books on Durkheim had been published in the meantime, heralding a renaissance of studies (Lukes 1988: X). In the case of Weber, the translator of the Swedish edition of *Wirtschaft und Gesellschaft* wrote, in 1983, prior to the publication of Weber's own writings in *Gesamtausgabe*, that the list of secondary literature was approaching 3,000 works (Lundquist 1983: IX). Some ten years later, on the threshold of the 1990s, a Danish Weberologist made the assessment that a single person concentrating, not on works on Weber's methodology, but only on his concept of the ideal type, would hardly be able to gain an overview of the field at all (Jacobsen 1991: 106). And, in a relatively recent bibliography, the author – who admits in the introduction to not having produced an exhaustive bibliography – fills roughly 275 pages with at least 4,000 almost exclusively English titles analysing Weber (Sica 2004: 1, 45–81, 93–334).

11 In this connection, it ought to be mentioned that the presentation in the following chapters of Weber's and Durkheim's views on social ontology, epistemology, value issues, etc. is steered by an interest in carrying out a systematic comparative analysis, as opposed to internal connections in their own works. Moreover, the approach chosen here, as well as the ambition of the analysis of Weber's and Durkheim's methodological views, does not provide a particularly satisfying basis for a position in discussions of the various interpretations, which Weber's methodological writings in particular have triggered among Weberologists. A number of examples of different Weberologists' interpretations can appropriately be read in relation to the ideal type concept. Jacobsen (1991: 116 ff.) points towards the neo-Kantian Friedrich Albert Lange as a likely source of inspiration for both the ideal type concept and the category of 'adequate causation' (*adäkvate Verursachung*) as communicative vessels and would appear to present 'historical individual' and ideal type partly in opposition to one another, such that the former is a static delimitation of the object at the processing stage, while the latter is a dynamic concept tailored for causal analysis. On the basis of a systematic consideration of the consistency, Schmid (1994) interprets the ideal type partly as a concept and partly as a hypothesis and is of the opinion that this interpretation is compatible with at least parts of Weber's own – according to Schmid – inconsistent formulations (Schmid 1994: 417 ff.). Aron (1968) interprets Weber, although without precise references, as operating with at least three kinds of ideal type, which must be seen in context with Weber's views on history and sociology and with various epistemological aspects in Weber (Aron 1968: 202–4, cf. 201). Von Schelting, who wonders how the ideal type concept has come to be regarded as one of Weber's great scientific achievements, regards Weber as being so unclear on this point that any attempt at cancelling out his lack of clarity, contradictions and ambiguities on this point will remain fruitless;

in order to be unambiguous, Weber should have reserved the ideal type concept for general-abstract constructions of rational action, as best known from economics (von Schelting 1934: 329 ff.). Eliaeson (1988), in line with von Schelting, expressly draws attention to the unclear content and status of the ideal type concept in Weber and sees the ideal type as Weber's response to the debates on values, on the use of methods from the natural sciences in the cultural and social sciences and, particularly, on economic method (the *Methodenstreit*), where the latter point is a response to Menger (Eliaeson 1988: 208 ff., cf. Eliaeson 2002: 48). Bruun (1972) has presented an in-depth, standard reference work about the value issue in Weber and places Weber's perception of the ideal type in context with his perception of values (Bruun 1972: 215 ff.), from the perspective that his texts do not, in principle, exclude the opportunity to provide a consistent interpretation of his ideal type concept; this is coupled together with 'value relation' (*Wertbeziehung*), value analysis and the explanation of behaviour, as well as partly also with Rickert's approach, although Weber oversteps this; and Bruun would not appear to operate as firmly with different types of ideal type, speaking instead about various variations or types of ideal type, depending on whether and how they can be coupled to value analysis in connection with behaviour (Bruun 1972: 202 ff.). In the 'Introduction' to Bruun 2007, which is a new edition of Bruun 1972, Bruun presents and reviews at least another two new and quite different interpretations of Weber's ideal type concept (Bruun 2007: 43–6).

2 Analysing Protestants and Catholics

1 Comment savoir quel mobile a déterminé l'agent et si, quand il a pris sa résolution, c'est la mort même qu'il voulait ou s'il avait quelque autre but ? L'intention est chose trop intime pour pouvoir être atteinte du dehors autrement que par de grossières approximations. Elle se dérobe même à l'observation intérieure.

(*LS*: 4)

2 En effet, si, au lieu de n'y voir que des événements particuliers, isolés les uns des autres et qui demandent à être examinés chacun à part, on considère l'ensemble des suicides commis dans une société donnée pendant une unité de temps donnée, on constate que le total ainsi obtenu n'est pas une simple somme d'unités indépendantes, un tout de collection, mais qu'il constitue par lui-même un fait nouveau et *sui generis*, qui a son unité et son individualité, sa nature propre par conséquent, et que, de plus, cette nature est éminemment sociale.

(*LS*: 8)

3 'On appelle suicide tout cas de mort qui résulte directement ou indirectement d'un acte positif ou négatif, accompli par la victime elle-même et qu'elle savait devoir produire ce résultat' (*LS*: 5).

Notes 99

4 'Si l'on veut savoir de quels confluents divers résulte le suicide considéré comme phénomène collectif, c'est sous sa forme collective, c'est-à-dire à travers les données statistiques, qu'il faut, dès l'abord, l'envisager' (*LS*: 143).

5 Le suicide égoïste vient de ce que les hommes n'aperçoivent plus de raison d'être à la vie ; le suicide altruiste de ce que cette raison leur paraît être en dehors de la vie elle-même ; la troisième sorte de suicide, dont nous venons de constater l'existence, de ce que leur activité est déréglée et de ce qu'ils en souffrent. En raison de son origine, nous donnerons à cette dernière espèce le nom de *suicide anomique*.

(*LS*: 288)

6 Si l'on jette un coup d'œil sur la carte des suicides européens, on reconnaît à première vue que dans les pays purement catholiques, comme l'Espagne, le Portugal, l'Italie, le suicide est très peu développé, tandis qu'il est à son maximum dans les pays protestant, en Prusse, en Saxe, en Danemark.

(*LS*: 149)

7 Si elle [la religion, HJ] protège l'homme contre le désir de se détruire, ce n'est pas parce qu'elle lui prêche, avec des arguments *sui generis*, le respect de sa personne ; c'est parce qu'elle est une société. Ce qui constitue cette société, c'est l'existence d'un certain nombre de croyances et de pratiques communes à tous les fidèles, traditionnelles et, par suite, obligatoires. Plus ces états collectifs sont nombreux et forts, plus la communauté religieuse est fortement intégrée ; plus aussi elle a de vertu préservatrice. Le détail des dogmes et des rites est secondaire. L'essentiel, c'est qu'ils soient de nature à alimenter une vie collective d'une suffisante intensité. Et c'est parce que l'Eglise protestante n'a pas le même degré de consistance que les autres, qu'elle n'a pas sur le suicide la même action modératrice.

(*LS*: 173)

8 'Tant il est vrai que le suicide dépend principalement, non des qualités congénitales des individus, mais des causes qui leur sont extérieures et qui les dominent !' (*LS*: 201–2).

9 De tous ces faits il résulte que le taux social des suicides ne s'explique que sociologiquement. C'est la constitution morale de la société qui fixe à chaque instant le contingent des morts volontaires. Il existe donc pour chaque peuple une force collective, d'une énergie déterminée, qui pousse les hommes à se tuer. Les mouvements que le patient accomplit et qui, au premier abord, paraissent n'exprimer que son tempérament personnel, sont, en réalité, la suite et le prolongement d'un état social qu'ils manifestent extérieurement.

Ainsi se trouve résolue la question que nous nous sommes posée au début de ce travail. Ce n'est pas par métaphore qu'on dit de chaque société humaine qu'elle a pour le suicide une aptitude plus ou moins prononcée : l'expression est fondée dans la nature des choses. Chaque groupe social a réellement pour cet acte un penchant collectif qui lui est propre et dont les penchants individuels dérivent, loin qu'il procède de ces derniers. Ce qui le constitue, ce sont ces courants d'égoïsme, d'altruisme ou d'anomie qui travaillent la société considérée, avec les tendances à la mélancolie langoureuse ou au renoncement actif ou à la lassitude exaspérée qui en sont les conséquences. Ce sont ces tendances de la collectivité qui, en pénétrant les individus, les déterminent à se tuer.

(*LS*: 336)

10 Moreover, on a more speculative basis, Durkheim presents a number of mental states in individuals (apathy, melancholy, etc.) corresponding to the three main types of suicide (*LS*: 314–26, 332). Durkheim also studies the relationship between the three suicide types and different ways of committing suicide (hanging, drowning, shooting, poison, etc.) and concludes, on the basis of the statistics, that the choice of method has more to do with nationality than with the type of suicide (*LS*: 329).

11 Weber's '*Vorbemerkung*' is written to '*Gesammelte Aufsätze zur Religions-soziologie*', which was published posthumously shortly after Weber's death in 1920 and includes 'The Protestant ethic and the spirit of capitalism', which is from 1904–5.

12 Der Grund des verschiedenen Verhaltens muß also der Hauptsache nach in der dauernden inneren Eigenart und *nicht* nur in der jeweiligen äußeren historisch-politischen Lage der Konfessionen gesucht werden . . .

Es würde also darauf ankommen, zunächst einmal zu untersuchen, welches diejenigen Elemente jener Eigenart der Konfessionen sind oder waren, die in der vorstehend geschilderten Richtung gewirkt haben und teilweise noch wirken.

(*DPE*: 33)

13 D.h. ein Komplex von Zusammenhängen in der geschichtlichen Wirklichkeit, die wir unter dem Gesichtspunkte ihrer *Kulturbedeutung* begrifflich zu einem Ganzen zusammenschließen.

Ein solcher historischer Begriff aber kann, da er inhaltlich sich auf eine in ihrer individuellen *Eigenart* bedeutungsvolle Erscheinung bezieht, nicht nach dem Schema: 'genus proximum, differentia specifica' definiert (zu deutsch: 'abgegrenzt'), sondern er muß aus seinen einzelnen, der geschichtlichen Wirklichkeit zu entnehmenden Bestandteilen allmählich *komponiert* werden.

(*DPE*: 39)

14 Damit jene der Eigenart des Kapitalismus angepaßte Art der Lebens-führung und Berufsauffassung 'ausgelesen' werden, d.h.: über andere den Sieg davontragen konnte, mußte sie offenbar zunächst *entstanden* sein, und zwar nicht in einzelnen isolierten Individuen, sondern als eine Anschauungsweise, die von Menschen*gruppen* getragen wurde. Diese Entstehung ist also das eigentlich zu Erklärende.

(*DPE*: 45–6)

Notes   101

15 'In ihrer pathetischen Unmenschlichkeit mußte diese Lehre nun für die Stimmung einer Generation, die sich ihrer grandiosen Konsequenz ergab, vor allem eine Folge haben: das Gefühl einer unerhörten *Vereinsamung des einzelnen Individuums*' (*DPE*: 122).

16 Wie wurde diese Lehre *ertragen* . . . in einer Zeit, welcher das Jenseits nicht nur wichtiger, sondern in vieler Hinsicht auch sicherer war als alle Interessen des diesseitigen Lebens? . . . Die eine Frage mußte ja alsbald für jeden einzelnen Gläubigen entstehen und alle anderen Interessen in den Hintergrund drängen: Bin *ich* denn erwählt? Und wie kann *ich* dieser Erwählung sicher werden?

(*DPE*: 127)

17 Die innerweltliche protestantische Askese – so können wir das bisher Gesagte wohl zusammenfassen – wirkte also mit voller Wucht gegen den unbefangenen *Genuß* des Besitzes, sie schnürte die *Konsumtion*, speziell die Luxuskonsumtion, ein. Dagegen *entlastete* sie im psychologischen Effekt den *Gütererwerb* von den Hemmungen der traditionalistischen Ethik, sie sprengte die Fesseln des Gewinnstrebens, indem sie es nicht nur legalisierte, sondern (in dem dargestellten Sinn) direkt als gottgewollt ansah.

(*DPE*: 179)

18 Auf der *Seite der Produktion* des priwatwirtschaftlichen Reichtums kämpfte die Askese gegen Unrechtlichkeit ebenso wie gegen rein *triebhafte* Habgier . . . Sondern was noch wichtiger war: die religiöse Wertung der rastlosen, stetigen, systematischen, weltlichen Berufsarbeit als schlechthin höchsten asketischen Mittels und zugleich sicherster und sichtbarster Bewährung des wiedergeborenen Menschen und seiner Glaubensechtheit mußte ja der denkbar mächtigste Hebel der Expansion jener Lebensauffassung sein, die wir hier als 'Geist' des Kapitalismus bezeichnet haben . . . Und halten wir nun noch jene Einschnürung der Konsumtion mit dieser Entfesselung des Erwerbsstrebens *zusammen*, so ist das äußere Ergebnis naheliegend: *Kapitalbildung* durch *asketischen Sparzwang*. Die Hemmungen, welche dem konsumtiven Verbrauch des Erworbenen entgegenstanden, mußten ja seiner produktiven Verwendung: als *Anlage*kapital, zugute kommen.

(*DPE*: 180)

19 Das Seelenheil und dies allein war der Angelpunkt ihres Lebens und Wirkens. Ihre ethischen Ziele und die praktischen Wirkungen ihrer Lehre waren alle hier verankert und nur *Konsequenzen* rein religiöser Motive. Und wir werden deshalb darauf gefaßt sein müssen, daß die Kulturwirkungen der Reformation zum guten Teil – vielleicht sogar für unsere speziellen Gesichtspunkte überwiegend – unvorhergesehene und geradezu *ungewollte* Folgen der Arbeit der Reformatoren waren, oft weit abliegend oder geradezu im Gegensatz stehend zu allem, was ihnen selbst vorschwebte.

(*DPE*: 75–6)

102 Notes

3 'Social ontology'

1 This is not to say that there is talk of social ontology in the form of in-depth reflections regarding the necessary character of being or which substance or elements the world is basically made up of. Nor is there talk of social ontology as it is traditionally found in continental philosophy, tied to the question regarding the relationship to 'the other', cf. e.g. Theunissen (1965: 6–7). Especially as far as Weber is concerned, it would also be strange – insofar as Weber is affected by Kantianism – if Weber did not stick to phenomena, or '*das Ding für sich*', as opposed to noumena, or '*das Ding an sich*'. Nevertheless, it is possible to find more or less 'social-ontological' statements in Weber about how reality meets the individual. Here, it matters less whether these statements are to be read as more fundamental ontological claims or merely as arguments for his views. What is significant here is that Weber presents such views, which can be reasonably characterized as being of more or less social-ontological character.

2 Die Sozialwissenschaft, die *wir* treiben wollen, ist eine *Wirklichkeitswissenschaft*. Wir wollen die uns umgebende Wirklichkeit des Lebens, in welches wir hineingestellt sind, *in ihrer Eigenart* verstehen – den Zusammenhang und die Kultur*bedeutung* ihrer einzelnen Erscheinungen in ihrer heutigen Gestaltung einerseits, die Gründe ihres geschichtlichen So-und-nicht-anders-Gewordenseins andererseits. Nun bietet uns das Leben, sobald wir uns auf die Art, in der es uns unmittelbar entgegentritt, zu besinnen suchen, eine schlechthin unendliche Mannigfaltigkeit von nach- und nebeneinander auftauchenden und vergehenden Vorgängen, 'in' uns und 'außer' uns.

(*GAW*/II: 170–1)

3 Endlos wälzt sich der Strom des unermeßlichen Geschehens der Ewigkeit entgegen. Immer neu und anders gefärbt bilden sich die Kulturprobleme, welche die Menschen bewegen, flüssig bleibt damit der Umkreis dessen, was aus jenem stets gleich unendlichen Strome des Individuellen Sinn und Bedeutung für uns erhält, 'historisches Individuum' wird.

(*GAW*/II: 184)

4 In dieses Chaos bringt *nur* der Umstand Ordnung, daß in jedem Fall nur ein Teil der individuellen Wirklichkeit für uns Interesse und *Bedeutung* hat, weil nur er in Beziehung steht zu den *Kulturwertideen*, mit welchen wir an die Wirklichkeit herantreten.

(*GAW*/II: 177–8)

5 'Alle Erkenntnis der Kulturwirklichkeit ist . . . stets eine Erkenntnis unter spezifisch besonderten Gesichtspunkten' (*GAW*: 181).

6 '"Kultur" ist ein vom Standpunkt des *Menschen* aus mit Sinn und Bedeutung bedachter endlicher Ausschnitt aus der sinnlosen Unendlichkeit des Weltgeschehens' (*GAW*/II: 180).

7 Transzendentale Voraussetzung jeder *Kulturwissenschaft* ist *nicht* etwa, daß wir eine bestimmte oder überhaupt irgend eine 'Kultur' *wertvoll* finden,

Notes 103

sondern daß wir Kultur*menschen sind*, begabt mit der Fähigkeit und dem Willen, bewußt zur Welt *Stellung* zu nehmen und ihr einen *Sinn* zu verleihen.

(*GAW*/II: 180)

8 Ce n'est donc pas en les [notions idéologiques, HJ] élaborant, de quelque manière qu'on s'y prenne, que l'on arrivera jamais à découvrir les lois de la réalité. Elles sont, au contraire, comme un voile qui s'interpose entre les choses et nous et qui nous les masque d'autant mieux qu'on le croit plus transparent.

Non seulement une telle science ne peut être que tronquée, mais elle manque de matière où elle puisse s'alimenter.

(*LRLMS*: 16)

9 Voilà donc un ordre de faits qui présentent des caractères très spéciaux : ils consistent en des manières d'agir, de penser et de sentir, extérieures à l'individu, et qui sont douées d'un pouvoir de coercition en vertu duquel ils s'imposent à lui.

(*LRLMS*: 5)

10 Elle [la vie sociale, HJ] consiste alors en libres courants qui sont perpétuellement en voie de transformation et que le regard de l'observateur ne parvient pas à fixer. C'est dire que ce côté n'est pas celui par où le savant peut aborder l'étude de la réalité sociale. Mais nous savons qu'elle présente cette particularité que, sans cesser d'être elle-même, elle est susceptible de se cristalliser. En dehors des actes individuels qu'elles suscitent, les habitudes collectives s'expriment sous des formes définies, règles juridiques, morales, dictons populaires, faits de structure sociale, etc. Comme ces formes existent d'une manière permanente, qu'elles ne changent pas avec les diverses applications qui en sont faites, elles constituent un objet fixe, un étalon constant qui est toujours à la portée de l'observateur et qui ne laisse pas de place aux impressions subjectives et aux observations personnelles.

(*LRLMS*: 44–5)

11 'En effet, pour les sociétés comme pour les individus, la santé est bonne et désirable, la maladie, au contraire, est la chose mauvaise et qui doit être évitée' (*LRLMS*: 49).

4 Epistemology

1 La sociologie n'est donc l'annexe d'aucune autre science ; elle est elle-même une science distincte et autonome, et le sentiment de ce qu'a de spécial la réalité sociale est même tellement nécessaire au sociologue que, seule, une culture spécialement sociologique peut le préparer à l'intelligence des faits sociaux.

(*LRLMS*: 143)

2 Puisque c'est par la sensation que l'extérieur des choses nous est donné, on peut donc dire en résumé : la science, pour être objective, doit partir, non

104 Notes

de concepts qui se sont formés sans elle, mais de la sensation . . . C'est de la sensation que se dégagent toutes les idées générales, vraies ou fausses, scientifiques ou non. Le point de départ de la science ou connaissance spéculative ne saurait donc être autre que celui de la connaissance vulgaire ou pratique. C'est seulement au delà, dans la manière dont cette matière commune est ensuite élaborée, que les divergences commencent.

(*LRLMS*: 43)

3 En procédant de cette manière, le sociologue, dès sa première démarche, prend immédiatement pied dans la réalité. En effet, la façon dont les faits sont ainsi classés ne dépend pas de lui, de la tournure particulière de son esprit, mais de la nature des choses.

(*LRLMS*: 36)

4 'Dès qu'on a prouvé que, dans un certain nombre de cas, deux phénomènes varient l'un comme l'autre, on peut être certain qu'on se trouve en présence d'une loi' (*LRLMS*: 132).

5 'Für die Soziologie (im hier gebrauchten Wortsinn, ebenso wie für die Geschichte) ist aber gerade der *Sinn*zusammenhang des Handelns Objekt der Erfassung' (*GAW*/XI: 552).

6 'Die Soziologie hat es eben keineswegs *nur* mit "sozialem Handeln" zu tun, sondern dieses bildet nur (für die hier betriebene Art von Soziologie) ihren zentralen Tatbestand, denjenigen, der für sie als Wissenschaft sozusagen *konstitutiv* ist' (*GAW*/XI: 565).

7 Die Qualität eines Vorganges als 'sozial-ökonomischer' Erscheinung ist nun nicht etwas, was ihm als solchem 'objektiv' anhaftet. Sie ist vielmehr bedingt durch die Richtung unseres Erkenntnis*interesses*, wie sie sich aus der spezifischen Kulturbedeutung ergibt, die wir dem betreffenden Vorgange im einzelnen Fall beilegen.

(*GAW*/II: 161)

8 Nicht die '*sachlichen*' Zusammenhänge der '*Dinge*', sondern die *gedanklichen* Zusammenhänge der *Probleme* liegen den Arbeitsgebieten der Wissenschaften zugrunde: wo mit neuer Methode einem neuen Problem nachgegangen wird und dadurch Wahrheiten entdeckt werden, welche neue bedeutsame Gesichtspunkte eröffnen, da entsteht eine neue 'Wissenschaft'.

(*GAW*/II: 166)

9 Alle Erkenntnis der Kulturwirklichkeit ist . . . stets eine Erkenntnis unter spezifisch *besonderten Gesichtspunkten*. Wenn wir von dem Historiker und Sozialforscher als elementare Voraussetzung verlangen, daß er Wichtiges von Unwichtigem unterscheiden könne, und daß er für diese Unterscheidung die erforderlichen 'Gesichtspunkte' habe, so heißt das lediglich, daß er verstehen müsse, die Vorgänge der Wirklichkeit – bewußt oder unbewußt – auf universelle 'Kulturwerte' zu beziehen und danach *die* Zusammenhänge herauszuheben, welche für uns bedeutsam sind. Wenn

immer wieder die Meinung auftritt, jene Gesichtspunkt könnten dem 'Stoff selbst entnommen' werden, so entspringt das der naiven Selbsttäuschung des Fachgelehrten, der nicht beachtet, daß er von vornherein kraft der Wertideen, mit denen er unbewußt an den Stoff herangegangen ist, aus einer absoluten Unendlichkeit einen winzigen Bestandteil als *das* herausgehoben hat, auf dessen Betrachtung es ihm allein *ankommt* . . .

Die kulturwissenschaftliche Erkenntnis in unserem Sinn ist also insofern an 'subjektive' Voraussetzungen *gebunden*, als sie sich nur um diejenigen Bestandteile der Wirklichkeit kümmert, welche irgend eine – noch so indirekte – Beziehung zu Vorgängen haben, denen wir Kultur*bedeutung* beilegen.

(*GAW*/II: 181–2)

10 Es ist und bleibt – *darauf* kommt es für uns an – für alle Zeit ein unüberbrückbarer Unterschied, ob eine Argumentation sich an unser Gefühl und unsere Fähigkeit, für konkrete praktische Ziele oder für Kulturformen und Kulturinhalte uns zu begeistern, wendet, oder, wo einmal die Geltung ethischer Normen in Frage steht, an unser Gewissen, *oder* endlich an unser Vermögen und Bedürfnis, die empirische Wirklichkeit in einer Weise *denkend zu ordnen*, welche den Anspruch auf Geltung als Erfahrungswahrheit erhebt.

(*GAW*/II: 155)

5 Science and values

1 Es gibt *keine* schlechthin 'objektive' wissenschaftliche Analyse des Kulturlebens oder – was vielleicht etwas Engeres, für unsern Zweck aber sicher nichts wesentlich anderes bedeutet – der 'sozialen Erscheinungen' *unabhängig* von speziellen und 'einseitigen' Gesichtspunkten, nach denen sie – ausdrücklich oder stillschweigend, bewußt oder unbewußt – als Forschungsobjekt ausgewählt, analysiert und darstellend gegliedert werden.

(*GAW*/II: 170)

2 Es würde nun zu weit führen, nach diesen umständlichen Darlegungen von 'Selbstverständlichkeiten' hier auch noch zu erörtern, daß für andere Werte genau das gleiche gilt, wie für den Wert des Strebens nach wissenschaftlicher Erkenntnis. Es gibt schlechterdings keine Brücke, welche von der wirklich *nur* 'empirischen' Analyse der gegebenen Wirklichkeit mit den Mitteln kausaler Erklärung zur Feststellung oder Bestreitung der 'Gültigkeit' *irgend*eines Werturteils führt, und die Wundtschen Begriffe der 'schöpferischen Synthese', des 'Gesetzes' der stetigen 'Steigerung der psychischen Energie' usw. enthalten Werturteile vom reinsten Wasser.

(*GAW*/I: 61)

3 Denn es ist und bleibt wahr, daß eine methodisch korrekte wissenschaftliche Beweisführung auf dem Gebiete der Sozialwissenschaften, wenn sie ihren Zweck erreicht haben will, auch von einem Chinesen als richtig anerkannt

werden muß oder – richtiger gesagt – daß sie dieses, vielleicht wegen Materialmangels nicht voll erreichbare, Ziel jedenfalls *erstreben* muß, daß ferner auch die *logische* Analyse eines Ideals auf seinen Gehalt und auf seine letzten Axiome hin und die Aufzeigung der aus seiner Verfolgung sich logischer und praktischer Weise ergebenden Konsequenzen, wenn sie als gelungen gelten soll, auch für ihn gültig sein muß, – während ihm für unsere ethischen Imperative das 'Gehör' fehlen kann, und während er das Ideal selbst und die daraus fließenden konkreten *Wertungen* ablehnen kann und sicherlich oft ablehnen wird, ohne dadurch dem wissenschaftlichen Wert jener denkenden *Analyse* irgend zu nahe zu treten.

(*GAW*/II: 155–6)

4 'Eine empirische Wissenschaft vermag niemanden zu lehren, was er *soll*, sondern nur, was er *kann* und – unter Umständen – was er *will*' (*GAW*/II: 151).

5 Es steht jedermann frei, sich auch in Form einer historischen Darstellung als 'stellungnehmendes Subjekt' zur Geltung zu bringen, politische oder Kulturideale oder andere 'Werturteile' zu propagieren und zur Illustration der praktischen Bedeutung dieser und anderer, bekämpfter, Ideale das ganze Material der Geschichte zu verwenden, ganz ebenso wie Biologen oder Anthropologen gewisse 'Fortschritts'-Ideale sehr subjektiver Art oder philosophische Ueberzeugungen in ihre Untersuchungen hineintragen und damit natürlich nichts anderes tun, als jemand, der das ganze Rüstzeug naturwissenschaftlicher Erkenntnis zur erbaulichen Illustration etwa der 'Güte Gottes' verwertet. In jedem Fall redet aber dann nicht der Forscher, sondern der wertende Mensch, und wendet sich die Darlegung an wertende, nicht nur an theoretisch erkennende Subjekte.

(*GAW*/I: 90)

6 'Gegen diese *Vermischung, nicht* etwa gegen das Eintreten für die eigenen Ideale richten sich die vorstehenden Ausführungen. *Gesinnungslosigkeit* und *wissenschaftliche "Objektivität"* haben keinerlei innere Verwandtschaft' (*GAW*/II: 157).

7 'Was schließlich am allerentschiedensten bekämpft werden muß, ist die nicht seltene Vorstellung: der Weg zur Wissenschaftlichen "Objektivität" werde durch ein Abwägen der verschiedenen Wertungen gegeneinander und ein "staatsmännisches" Kompromiß zwischen ihnen betreten' (*GAW*/X: 499).

8 'Ceux [ordres des faits, HJ] qui sont tout ce qu'ils doivent être et ceux qui devraient être autrement qu'ils ne sont, les phénomènes normaux et les phénomènes pathologiques' (*LRLMS*: 47).

9 Encore ces spéculations abstraites ne constituent-elles pas une science, à parler exactement, puisqu'elles ont pour objet de déterminer non ce qui est, en fait, la règle suprême de la moralité, mais ce qu'elle doit être. De même, ce qui tient le plus de place dans les recherches des économistes, c'est la question de savoir, par exemple, si la société *doit être* organisée d'après les conceptions des individualistes ou d'après celles des socialistes ; *s'il est meilleur* que l'État intervienne dans les rapports industriels et commerciaux

Notes   107

ou les abandonne entièrement à l'initiative privée ; si le système monétaire *doit être* le monométallisme ou le bimétallisme, etc. etc. Les lois proprement dites y sont peu nombreuses ; même celles qu'on a l'habitude d'appeler ainsi ne méritent généralement pas cette qualification, mais ne sont que des maximes d'action, des préceptes pratiques déguisés. Voilà, par exemple, la fameuse loi de l'offre et de la demande. Elle n'a jamais été établie inductivement, comme expression de la réalité économique.

(*LRLMS*: 26)

10   D'après une théorie dont les partisans se recrutent dans les écoles les plus diverses, la science ne nous apprendrait rien sur ce que nous devons vouloir. Elle ne connaît, dit-on, que des faits qui ont tous la même valeur et le même intérêt ; elle les observe, les explique, mais ne les juge pas ; pour elle, il n'y en a point qui soient blâmables. Le bien et le mal n'existent à ses yeux. Elle peut bien nous dire comment les causes produisent leurs effets, non quelles fins doivent être poursuivies.

(*LRLMS*: 47)

11   La science se trouve ainsi destituée, ou à peu près, de toute efficacité pratique, et, par conséquent, sans grande raison d'être ; car à quoi bon se travailler pour connaître le réel, si la connaissance que nous en acquérons ne peut nous servir dans la vie ?

(*LRLMS*: 48)

12   Or, si la science ne peut nous aider dans le choix du but le meilleur, comment pourrait-elle nous apprendre quelle est la meilleure voie pour y parvenir ? Pour quoi nous recommanderait-elle la plus rapide de préférence à la plus économique, la plus sûre plutôt que la plus simple, ou inversement ? Si elle ne peut nous guider dans la détermination des fins supérieures, elle n'est pas moins impuissante quand il s'agit de ces fins secondaires et subordonnées que l'on appelle des moyens.

(*LRLMS*: 48)

13   En effet, pour les sociétés comme pour les individus, la santé est bonne et désirable, la maladie, au contraire, est la chose mauvaise et qui doit être évitée. Si donc nous trouvons un critère objectif, inhérent aux faits eux-mêmes, qui nous permette de distinguer scientifiquement la santé de la maladie dans les divers ordres de phénomènes sociaux, la science sera en état d'éclairer la pratique tout en restant fidèle à sa propre méthode.

(*LRLMS*: 49)

14   'Entre la science et l'art il n'y a plus un abîme ; mais on passe de l'une à l'autre sans solution de continuité' (*LRLMS*: 49).

15   Le devoir de l'homme d'État n'est plus de pousser violemment les sociétés vers un idéal qui lui paraît séduisant, mais son rôle est celui du médecin : il prévient l'éclosion des maladies par une bonne hygiène et, quand elles sont déclarées, il cherche à les guérir.

(*LRLMS*: 74–5)

108   Notes

6   Methodological individualism

1 Soziologie (im hier verstandenen Sinn dieses sehr vieldeutig gebrauchten Wortes) soll heißen: eine Wissenschaft, welche soziales Handeln deutend verstehen und dadurch in seinem Ablauf und seinen Wirkungen ursächlich erklären will. 'Handeln' soll dabei ein menschliches Verhalten (einerlei ob äußeres oder innerliches Tun, Unterlassen oder Dulden) heißen, wenn und insofern als der oder die Handelnden mit ihm einen subjektiven *Sinn* verbinden. 'Soziales' Handeln aber soll ein solches Handeln heißen, welches seinem von dem oder den Handelnden gemeinten Sinn nach auf das Verhalten *anderer* bezogen wird und daran in seinem Ablauf orientiert ist.

(*GAW*/XI: 542)

2 'Handeln [Handeln, HJ] im Sinn sinnhaft verständlicher Orientierung des eignen Verhaltens gibt es für uns stets nur als Verhalten von einer oder mehreren *einzelnen* Personen' (*GAW*/XI: 552).

3 Für wiederum andere (z. B. juristische) Erkenntniszwecke oder für praktische Ziele kann es andererseits zweckmäßig und geradezu unvermeidlich sein: soziale Gebilde ('Staat', 'Genossenschaft', 'Aktiengesellschaft', 'Stiftung') genau so zu behandeln, wie Einzelindividuen (z.B. als Träger von Rechten und Pflichten oder als Täter *rechtlich* relevanter Handlungen). Für die verstehende Deutung des Handelns durch die Soziologie sind dagegen diese Gebilde lediglich Abläufe und Zusammenhänge spezifischen Handelns *einzelner* Menschen, da diese allein für uns verständliche Träger von sinnhaft orientiertem Handeln sind.

(*GAW*/XI: 552–3)

4 Zur Vermeidigung möglicher Mißverständnisse ein Wort. Die Gestalten von Kapitalist und Grundeigentümer zeichne ich keineswegs in rosigem Licht. Aber es handelt sich hier um die Personen nur, soweit sie die Personifikation ökonomischer Kategorien sind, Träger von bestimmten Klasseverhältnissen und Interessen.

(Marx 1962: 16)

The notion of *Träger* (carrier) has first and foremost been taken over and used by the Althusser School. With respect to methodological collectivism, the Althusser School is in line with Durkheim and certainly not with Weber. The notion of *Träger* would not normally be associated with methodological individualism, as it indicates that the individual has no insight into the context of social meaning in which the individual operates. This would be against Weber's view with respect to attempting to account for behaviour on the basis of the subjective meaning that it has for the individual.

5 Das Ziel der Betrachtung: 'Verstehen', ist schließlich auch der Grund, weshalb die verstehende Soziologie (in unserem Sinne) das Einzelindividuum und sein Handeln als unterste Einheit, als ihr 'Atom' – wenn der an sich bedenkliche Vergleich hier einmal erlaubt ist – behandelt. . . . Begriffe

wie 'Staat', 'Genossenschaft', 'Feudalismus' und ähnliche bezeichnen für die Soziologie, allgemein gesagt, Kategorien für bestimmte Arten menschlichen Zusammenhandelns, und es ist also ihre Aufgabe, sie auf 'verständliches' Handeln, und das heißt ausnahmslos: auf Handeln der beteiligten Einzelmenschen, zu reduzieren.

(*GAW*/VIII: 439)

6 Denn stets beginnt auch dort die entscheidende empirisch-soziologische Arbeit erst mit der Frage: welche Motive *bestimmten* und *bestimmen* die einzelnen Funktionäre und Glieder dieser 'Gemeinschaft', sich so zu verhalten, daß sie *entstand* und *fortbesteht*? Alle funktionale (vom 'Ganzen' ausgehende) Begriffsbildung leistet nur *V*orarbeit dafür, deren Nutzen und Unentbehrlichkeit – wenn sie richtig geleistet wird – natürlich unbestreitbar ist.

(*GAW*/XI: 558)

7 Ils constituent donc une espèce nouvelle et c'est à eux que doit être donnée et réservée la qualification de *sociaux*. Elle leur convient ; car il est clair que, n'ayant pas l'individu pour substrat, ils ne peuvent en avoir d'autre que la société, soit la société politique dans son intégralité, soit quelqu'un des groupes partiels qu'elle renferme, confessions religieuses, écoles politiques, littéraires, corporations professionnelles, etc.

(*LRLMS*: 5)

8 Mais on se méprendrait étrangement sur notre pensée, si, de ce qui précède, on tirait cette conclusion que la sociologie, suivant nous, doit ou même peut faire abstraction de l'homme et de ses facultés. Il est clair, au contraire, que les caractères généraux de la nature humaine entrent dans le travail d'élaboration d'où résulte la vie sociale. Seulement, ce n'est pas eux qui la suscitent ni qui lui donnent sa forme spéciale ; ils ne font que la rendre possible. Les représentations, les émotions, les tendances collectives n'ont pas pour causes génératrices certains états de la conscience des particuliers, mais les conditions où se trouve le corps social dans son ensemble. Sans doute, elles ne peuvent se réaliser que si les natures individuelles n'y sont pas réfractaires ; mais celles-ci ne sont que la matière indéterminée que le facteur social détermine et transforme.

(*LRLMS*: 105)

9 Mais, dira-t-on, un phénomène ne peut être collectif que s'il est commun à tous les membres de la société ou, tout au moins, à la plupart d'entre eux, partant, s'il est général. Sans doute, mais s'il est général, c'est parce qu'il est collectif (c'est-à-dire plus ou moins obligatoire), bien loin qu'il soit collectif parce qu'il est général. C'est un état du groupe, qui se répète chez les individus parce qu'il s'impose à eux. Il est dans chaque partie parce qu'il est dans le tout, loin qu'il soit dans le tout parce qu'il est dans les parties.

(*LRLMS*: 10)

110   Notes

10 'Les faits sociaux ne peuvent être expliqués que par des faits sociaux' (*LRLMS*: 147).

11 'Nous avons fait voir qu'un fait social ne peut être expliqué que par un autre fait social . . .' (*LRLMS*: 143).

12 '*La cause déterminante d'un fait social doit être cherchée parmi les faits sociaux antécédents, et non parmi les états de la conscience individuelle*' (*LRLMS*: 109).

7 Types of explanation

1 'On peut en effet, sans dénaturer le sens de cette expression, appeler *institution* toutes les croyances et tous les modes de conduite institués par la collectivité ; la sociologie peut alors être définie : la science des institutions, de leur genèse et de leur fonctionnement' (*LRLMS*: XXII).

2 '*La fonction d'un fait social doit toujours être recherchée dans le rapport qu'il soutient avec quelque fin sociale*' (*LRLMS*: 109).

3 C'est, du reste, une proposition vraie en sociologie comme en biologie que l'organe est indépendant de la fonction, c'est-à-dire que, tout en restant le même, il peut servir à des fins différentes. C'est donc que les causes qui le font être sont indépendantes des fins auxquelles il sert.

(*LRLMS*: 91)

4 '*Quand donc on entreprend d'expliquer un phénomène social, il faut rechercher séparément la cause efficiente qui le produit et la fonction qu'il remplit*' (*LRLMS*: 95).

5 '*A un même effet correspond toujours une même cause*' (*LRLMS*: 127).

6 Par exemple, on peut établir de la manière la plus certaine que la tendance au suicide varie comme la tendance à l'instruction. Mais il est impossible de comprendre comment l'instruction peut conduire au suicide ; une telle explication est en contradiction avec les lois de la psychologie. L'instruction, surtout réduite aux connaissances élémentaires, n'atteint que les régions les plus superficielles de la conscience ; au contraire, l'instinct de conservation est une de nos tendances fondamentales. Il ne saurait donc être sensiblement affecté par un phénomène aussi éloigné et d'un aussi faible retentissement. On en vient ainsi à se demander si l'un et l'autre fait ne seraient pas la conséquence d'un même état. Cette cause commune, c'est l'affaiblissement du traditionalisme religieux qui renforce à la fois le besoin de savoir et le penchant au suicide.

(*LRLMS*: 131)

7 Le groupe pense, sent, agit tout autrement que ne feraient ses membres, s'ils étaient isolés. Si donc on part de ces derniers, on ne pourra rien comprendre à ce qui se passe dans le groupe. En un mot, il y a entre la psychologie et la sociologie la même solution de continuité qu'entre la biologie et les sciences physico-chimiques. Par conséquent, toutes les fois qu'un phénomène social est directement expliqué par un phénomène psychique, on peut être assuré que l'explication est fausse.

(*LRLMS*: 103)

Notes 111

8 ‘*La cause déterminante d'un fait social doit être cherchée parmi les faits sociaux antécédents, et non parmi les états de la conscience individuelle*’ (*LRLMS*: 109).

9 ‘Soziologie (im hier verstandenen Sinn dieses sehr vieldeutig gebrauchten Wortes) soll heißen: eine Wissenschaft, welche soziales Handeln deutend verstehen und dadurch in seinem Ablauf und seinen Wirkungen ursächlich erklären will’ (*GAW*/XI: 542).

10 ‘Jede denkende Besinnung auf die letzten Elemente sinnvollen menschlichen Handelns ist zunächst gebunden an die Kategorien "Zweck" und "Mittel"’ (*GAW*/II: 149).

11 ‘Die unmittelbar "verständlichste Art" der sinnhaften Struktur eines Handelns ist ja das subjektiv streng rational orientierte Handeln nach Mitteln, welche (subjektiv) für eindeutig adäquat zur Erreichung von (subjektiv) eindeutig und klar erfaßten Zwecken gehalten werden’ (*GAW*/VIII: 432).

12 ‘"Zweck" ist für *unsere* Betrachtung die Vorstellung eines *Erfolges*, welche *Ursache* einer Handlung wird; wie *jede* Ursache, welche zu einem *bedeutungsvollen* Erfolg beiträgt oder beitragen kann, so berücksichtigen wir auch diese’ (*GAW*/II: 183).

13 ‘"Erklären" bedeutet also für eine mit dem Sinn des Handelns befasste Wissenschaft soviel wie: Erfassung des Sinn*zusammenhangs*, in den, seinem subjektiv gemeinten Sinn nach, ein aktuell verständliches Handeln hineingehört’ (*GAW*/XI: 547).

14 Wogegen sich die Soziologie aber auflehnen würde, wäre die Annahme: daß ‘Verstehen’ und kausales ‘Erklären’ *keine* Beziehung zueinander hätten, so richtig es ist, daß sie durchaus am entgegengesetzten Pol des Geschehens mit ihrer Arbeit beginnen, insbesondere die statistische Häufigkeit eines Sichverhaltens dieses um keine Spur sinnhaft ‘verständlicher’ macht und optimale ‘Verständlichkeit’ als solche gar nichts für die Häufigkeit besagt, bei absoluter subjektiver Zweckrationalität sogar meist gegen sie spricht.
(*GAW*/VIII: 436–7)

15 Unsere eigentliche Frage ist ja nun aber: durch welche logischen Operationen gewinnen wir die Einsicht und vermögen wir sie demonstrierend zu begründen, *daß* eine solche Kausalbeziehung zwischen jenen ‘wesentlichen’ Bestandteilen des Erfolges und bestimmten Bestandteilen aus der Unendlichkeit determinierender Momente vorliegt. Offenbar nicht durch einfache ‘Beobachtung’ des Herganges . . . Sondern die kausale Zurechnung vollzieht sich in Gestalt eines Gedankenprozesses, welcher eine Serie von *Abstraktionen* enthält. Die erste und entscheidende ist nun eben die, daß wir von den tatsächlich kausalen Komponenten des Verlaufs eine oder einige in bestimmter Richtung abgeändert *denken* und uns fragen, ob unter den dergestalt abgeänderten Bedingungen des Hergangs der (in den ‘wesentlichen’ Punkten) gleiche Erfolg oder *welcher andere* ‘zu erwarten gewesen’ wäre.
(*GAW*/III: 273)

16 ‘Um die wirklichen Kausalzusammenhänge zu durchschauen, *konstruieren wir unwirkliche*’ (*GAW*/III: 287).

112   Notes

17 Kausale Erklärung bedeutet also die Feststellung: daß nach einer irgendwie abschätzbaren, im – seltenen – Idealfall: zahlenmäßig angebbaren, Wahrscheinlichkeits*regel* auf einen bestimmten beobachteten (inneren oder äußeren) Vorgang ein bestimmter anderer Vorgang folgt (oder: mit ihm gemeinsam auftritt).

Eine *richtige kausale Deutung* eines konkreten Handelns bedeutet: daß der äußere Ablauf und das Motiv *zutreffend* und zugleich in ihrem Zusammenhang sinnhaft *verständlich* erkannt sind. Eine richtige kausale Deutung *typischen* Handelns (verständlicher Handlungstypus) bedeutet: daß der als typisch behauptete Hergang sowohl (in irgendeinem Grade) sinnadäquat erscheint wie (in irgendeinem Grade) als kausaladäquat festgestellt werden kann. Fehlt die Sinnadäquanz, dann liegt selbst bei größter und zahlenmäßig in ihrer Wahrscheinlichkeit präzis angebbarer Regelmäßigkeit des Ablaufs (des äußeren sowohl wie des psychischen) nur eine *unverstehbare* (oder nur unvollkommen verstehbare) *statistische* Wahrscheinlichkeit vor. Andererseits bedeutet für die Tragweite soziologischer Erkenntnisse selbst die evidenteste Sinnadäquanz nur in dem Maß eine richtige *kausale* Aussage, als der Beweis für das Bestehen einer (irgendwie angebbaren) *Chance* erbracht wird, daß das Handeln den sinnadäquat erscheinenden Verlauf *tatsächlich* mit angebbarer Häufigkeit oder Annäherung (durchschnittlich oder im 'reinen' Fall) zu nehmen *pflegt*. Nur solche statistische Regelmäßigkeiten, welche einem *verständlichen* gemeinten Sinn eines sozialen Handelns entsprechen, sind (im hier gebrauchten Wortsinn) verständliche Handlungstypen, also: 'soziologische Regeln'.

(*GAW*/XI: 550–1)

8 Formation of concepts

1 Er wird gewonnen durch einseitige *Steigerung eines* oder *einiger* Gesichtspunkte und durch Zusammenschluß einer Fülle von diffus und diskret, hier mehr, dort weniger, stellenweise gar nicht, vorhandenen *Einzel*erscheinungen, die sich jenen einseitig, herausgehobenen Gesichtspunkten fügen, zu einem in sich einheitlichen *Gedanken*bilde.

(*GAW*/II: 191)

2 Es gibt Idealtypen von Bordellen so gut wie von Religionen, und es gibt von den ersteren sowohl Idealtypen von solchen, die vom Standpunkt der heutigen Polizeiethik aus technisch 'zweckmäßig' erscheinen würden, wie von solchen, bei denen das gerade Gegenteil der Fall ist.

(*GAW*/II: 200)

3 'In seiner begrifflichen Reinheit ist dieses Gedankenbild nirgends in der Wirklichkeit empirisch vorfindbar, es ist eine *Utopie*' (*GAW*/II: 191).

4 Nichts aber ist allerdings gefährlicher als die, naturalistischen Vorurteilen entstammende, *Vermischung* von Theorie und Geschichte, sei es in der Form,

Notes 113

daß man glaubt, in jenen theoretischen Begriffsbildern den 'eigentlichen' Gehalt, das 'Wesen' der geschichtlichen Wirklichkeit fixiert zu haben, oder daß man sie als ein Prokrustesbett benutz, in welches die Geschichte hineingezwängt werden soll, oder daß man gar die 'Ideen' als eine hinter der Flucht der Erscheinungen stehende 'eigentliche' Wirklichkeit, als reale 'Kräfte' hypostasiert, die sich in der Geschichte auswirkten.

(*GAW*/II: 195)

5 Alle Darstellungen eines '*Wesens*' des Christentums z. B. sind Idealtypen von stets und notwendig nur sehr relativer und problematischer Gültigkeit, wenn sie als historische Darstellung des empirisch Vorhandenen angesehen sein wollen, dagegen von hohem heuristischen [heuristischem, HJ] Wert für die Forschung und hohem systematischem Wert für die Darstellung, wenn sie lediglich als begriffliche Mittel zur *Vergleichung* und *Messung* der Wirklichkeit an ihnen verwendet werden.

(*GAW*/II: 198–9)

6 Um z.B. die Führung eines Krieges zu 'verstehen', muß unvermeidlich – wenn auch nicht notwendig ausdrücklich oder in ausgeführter Form – beiderseits ein idealer Feldherr vorgestellt werden, dem die Gesamtsituation und Dislokation der beiderseitigen militärischen Machtmittel und die sämtlichen daraus sich ergebenden Möglichkeiten, das in concreto eindeutige Ziel: Zertrümmerung der gegnerischen Militärmacht, zu erreichen, bekannt und stets gegenwärtig gewesen wären, und der auf Grund dieser Kenntnis irrtumslos und auch logisch 'fehlerfrei' gehandelt hätte. Denn nur dann kann eindeutig festgestellt werden, welchen kausalen Einfluß der Umstand, daß die wirklichen Feldherren weder jene Kenntnis noch diese Irrtumslosigkeit besaßen und daß sie überhaupt keine bloß rationalen Denkmaschinen waren, auf den Gang der Dinge gehabt hat. Die rationale Konstruktion hat also hier den Wert, als Mittel richtiger kausaler 'Zurechnung' zu fungieren.

(*GAW*/X: 534)

7 'Denn Zweck der idealtypischen Begriffsbildung ist es überall, *nicht* das Gattungsmäßige, sondern umgekehrt die *Eigenart* von Kulturerscheinungen scharf zum Bewußtsein zu bringen' (*GAW*/II: 202).

8 'Eine "Definition" jener Synthesen des historischen Denkens nach dem Schema: genus proximum, differentia specifica ist natürlich ein Unding: man mache doch die Probe' *(GAW*/II: 194).

9 Toute investigation scientifique porte sur un groupe déterminé de phénomènes qui répondent à une même définition. La première démarche du sociologue doit donc être de définir les choses dont il traite, afin que l'on sache et qu'il sache bien de quoi il est question. C'est la première et la plus indispensable condition de toute preuve et de toute vérification ; une théorie, en effet, ne peut être contrôlée que si l'on sait reconnaître les faits dont elle doit rendre compte.

(*LRLMS*: 34)

114   Notes

10 'Ne jamais prendre pour objet de recherches qu'un groupe de phénomènes préalablement définis par certains caractères extérieurs qui leur sont communs et comprendre dans la même recherche tous ceux qui répondent à cette définition' (*LRLMS*: 35).

11 'Les caractères extérieurs en fonction desquels il définit l'objet de ses recherches doivent être aussi objectifs que possible' (*LRLMS*: 44).

12 'Une règle de droit est ce qu'elle est et il n'y a pas deux manières de la percevoir' (*LRLMS*: 45).

9   Laws

1 '*A un même effet correspond toujours une même cause*' (*LRLMS*: 127).

2 'Or il n'y a que les philosophes qui aient jamais mis en doute l'intelligibilité de la relation causale. Pour le savant, elle ne fait pas question ; elle est supposée par la méthode de la science' (*LRLMS*: 126).

3 Tout ce qu'elle [la sociologie, HJ] demande qu'on lui accorde, c'est que le principe de causalité s'applique aux phénomènes sociaux. Encore ce principe est-il posé par elle, non comme une nécessité rationnelle, mais seulement comme un postulat empirique, produit d'une induction légitime. Puisque la loi de causalité a été vérifiée dans les autres règnes de la nature, que, progressivement, elle a étendu son empire du monde physico-chimique au monde biologique, de celui-ci au monde psychologique, on est en droit d'admettre qu'elle est également vraie du monde social.

(*LRLMS*: 139–40)

4 'En pratiquant dans cet esprit le raisonnement expérimental, on aura beau réunir un nombre considérable de faits, on ne pourra jamais obtenir de lois précises, de rapports déterminés de causalités' (*LRLMS*: 127).

5 'Dès qu'on a prouvé que, dans un certain nombre de cas, deux phénomènes varient l'un comme l'autre, on peut être certain qu'on se trouve en présence d'une loi' (*LRLMS*: 132).

6 Quand deux phénomènes varient régulièrement l'un comme l'autre, il faut maintenir ce rapport alors même que, dans certain cas, l'un de ces phénomènes se présenterait sans l'autre. Car il peut se faire, ou bien que la cause ait été empêchée de produire son effet par l'action de quelque cause contraire, ou bien qu'elle se trouve présente, mais sous une forme différente de celle que l'on a précédemment observée. Sans doute, il y a lieu de voir, comme on dit, d'examiner les faits à nouveau, mais non d'abandonner sur-le-champ les résultats d'une démonstration régulièrement faite.

(*LRLMS*: 130)

7 Aussi, sa fameuse loi de trois états n'a-t-elle rien d'un rapport de causalité ; fût-elle exacte, elle n'est et ne peut être qu'empirique. C'est un coup d'œil sommaire sur l'histoire écoulée du genre humain. C'est tout à fait arbitrairement que Comte considère le troisième état comme l'état définitif de l'humanité. Qui nous dit qu'il n'en surgira pas un autre dans l'avenir ?

(*LRLMS*: 117–18)

Notes 115

8 Wo immer die kausale Erklärung einer 'Kulturerscheinung' . . . in Betracht kommt, da kann die Kenntnis von *Gesetzen* der Verursachung nicht *Zweck*, sondern nur *Mittel* der Untersuchung sein. Sie erleichtert und ermöglicht uns die kausale Zurechnung der in ihrer Individualität kulturbedeutsamen Bestandteile der Erscheinungen zu ihren konkreten Ursachen. Soweit, und nur soweit, als sie dies leistet, ist sie für die Erkenntnis individueller Zusammenhänge wertvoll. Und je 'allgemeiner', d.h. abstrakter, die Gesetze [sind], desto weniger leisten sie für die Bedürfnisse der kausalen Zurechnung *individueller* Erscheinungen und damit indirekt für das Verständnis der Bedeutung der Kulturvorgänge.

(*GAW*/II: 178)

9 *Nur* ist eben die Aufstellung solcher Regelmäßigkeiten nicht *Ziel*, sondern *Mittel* der Erkenntnis, und ob es Sinn hat, eine aus der Alltagserfahrung bekannte Regelmäßigkeit ursächlicher Verknüpfung als 'Gesetz' in eine Formel zu bringen, ist in jedem einzelnen Fall eine Zweckmäßigkeitsfrage. Für die exakte Naturwissenschaft sind die 'Gesetze' um so wichtiger und wertvoller, je *allgemeingültiger* sie sind; für die Erkenntnis der historischen Erscheinungen in ihrer konkreten Voraussetzung sind die *allgemeinsten* Gesetze, weil die inhaltleersten, regelmäßig auch die wertlosesten. Denn je umfassender die Geltung eines *Gattungs*begriffes – sein *Umfang* – ist, desto mehr führt er uns von der Fülle der Wirklichkeit *ab*, da er ja, *um* das Gemeinsame möglichst vieler Erscheinungen zu enthalten, möglichst abstrakt, also inhalts*arm* sein muß. Die Erkenntnis des Generellen ist uns in den Kulturwissenschaften nie um ihrer selbst willen wertvoll.

(*GAW*/II: 179–80)

10 Die Soziologie bildet – wie schon mehrfach als selbstverständlich vorausgesetzt – *Typen*-Begriffe und sucht *generelle* Regeln des Geschehens. Im Gegensatz zur Geschichte, welche die kausale Analyse und Zurechnung *individueller, kultur*wichtiger, Handlungen, Gebilde, Persönlichkeiten erstrebt. Die Begriffsbildung der Soziologie entnimmt ihr *Material*, als Paradigmata, sehr wesentlich, wenn auch keineswegs ausschließlich, den auch unter den Gesichtspunkten der Geschichte relevanten Realitäten des Handelns. Sie bildet ihre Begriffe und sucht nach ihren Regeln vor allem *auch* unter dem Gesichtspunkt: ob sie damit der historischen kausalen Zurechnung der kulturwichtigen Erscheinungen einen Dienst leisten kann. Wie bei jeder generalisierenden Wissenschaft bedingt die Eigenart ihrer Abstraktionen es, daß ihre Begriffe gegenüber der konkreten Realität des Historischen relativ inhalts*leer* sein müssen. Was sie dafür zu bieten hat, ist gesteigerte *Eindeutigkeit* der Begriffe. Diese gesteigerte Eindeutigkeit ist durch ein möglichstes Optimum von *Sinn*adäquanz erreicht, wie es die soziologische Begriffsbildung erstrebt. Diese kann – und das ist bisher vorwiegend berücksichtigt – bei *rationalen* (wert- und zweckrationalen) Begriffen und Regeln besonders vollständig erreicht werden. Aber die Soziologie sucht auch irrationale (mystische, prophetische, pneumatische, affektuelle) Erscheinungen in theoretischen und zwar *sinn*adäquaten Begriffen zu erfassen . . . Daß die Soziologie außerdem nach Gelegenheit

116 Notes

auch den *Durchschnitts*typus von der Art der empirisch-statistischen Typen verwendet: – ein Gebilde, welches der methodischen Erläuterung nicht besonders bedarf, versteht sich von selbst. Aber wenn sie von '*typischen*' Fällen spricht, meint sie im Zweifel stets den *Idealtypus*, der seinerseits rational oder irrational sein *kann*, zumeist (in der nationalökonomischen Theorie z. B. immer) rational ist, stets aber *sinn*adäquat konstruiert wird.

(*GAW/*XI: 559–60)

10 Weber and Durkheim: a methodological comparison

1 Without pursuing this issue much further, this distance between Weber and Durkheim becomes no less when placing them on their respective sides of the gap in classic societal theory between, respectively, agent-oriented (Weber) and structure-oriented (Durkheim) approaches. Giddens is renowned for having devoted attention to the question regarding the compatibility of agent-oriented and structure-oriented approaches (Giddens 1984a: 160–2, 1984b: 162). The picture is the same when relating them to common sense. Weber, emphasizing the meaning of behaviour, intentional explanations and causal explanations in terms of 'thought experiments' and counterfactual thinking, is closer to common sense than Durkheim, who stresses the necessity for science not to rely uncritically on common sense.

2 This conclusion is not new, but it is in line with e.g. Bendix (1980: 282–4, 297–8). Bendix holds true to the title of his article, 'Two sociological traditions', with his assessment that Weber and Durkheim are opposites with respect to theory and methodology to such a degree that they continue to represent two different traditions within sociology. Bendix, who is open to other points of view on this matter, assumes a position marked by traces of scepticism towards Parsons' convergence thesis (Bendix 1980: 283). Parsons' thesis is based on an interpretation of Weber and Durkheim as well as Marshall and Pareto, so that the divergence between them is toned down and made to make room for a construction – with Parsons himself as the constructor – of a voluntaristic theory of action that cumulatively builds further on Parsons' sociological predecessors (Parsons 1968: 719–20, cf. 698 ff.). Münch (2004), who, like Parsons, must be regarded as a convergence theoretician, has written a fictive dialogue between Weber and Durkheim. Although Münch naturally does most of the 'talking', it is hinted that their contemporary relevance – particularly in the case of Weber – is as part of a sociology-based meta-disciplinary language and analysis apparatus to be able to integrate various academic disciplines outside sociology. This thus renders it possible – in an adequate and cumulative manner – to analyse current issues such as European integration and globalization, which modern sociologists, according to Münch, do not manage to analyse satisfactorily (Münch 2004: 83–4, 102–3).

3 Nilsen (2003), a Norwegian analysis, provides an example of this kind of interpretation. The argument is that Weber's and Durkheim's approaches

Notes   117

are considerably closer to one another than is usually assumed, such that Weber must almost – more or less like Durkheim – be regarded as a moderate methodological collectivist, or at least a moderate methodological individualist. The argument includes a distinction between extreme and moderate variations of methodological individualism and collectivism (Nilsen 2003: 2–6, 15, 24, 34–5, 40, 53).

4   Die christliche Askese, anfangs aus der Welt in die Einsamkeit flüchtend, hatte bereits aus dem Kloster heraus, indem sie der Welt entsagte, die Welt kirchlich beherrscht. Aber dabei hatte sie im ganzen dem weltlichen Alltagsleben seinen natürlich unbefangenen Charakter gelassen. Jetzt trat sie auf den Markt des Lebens, schlug die Tür des Klosters hinter sich zu und unternahm es, gerade das weltliche *Alltags*leben mit ihrer Methodik zu durchtränken, es zu einem rationalen Leben *in* der Welt und doch *nicht von* dieser Welt oder *für* diese Welt umzugestalten. Mit welchem Ergebnis, wollen unsere weiteren Darlegungen zu zeigen versuchen.

(*DPE*: 165)

5   Die Frage nach den Triebkräften der Expansion des modernen Kapitalismus ist nicht in erster Linie eine Frage nach der Herkunft der kapitalistisch verwertbaren Geldvorräte, sondern vor allem nach der Entwicklung des kapitalistischen Geistes. Wo er auflebt und sich auszuwirken vermag, *verschafft* er sich die Geldvorräte als Mittel seines Wirkens, nicht aber umgekehrt.

(*DPE*: 58)

6   'C'est une loi générale que les minorités religieuses, pour pouvoir se maintenir plus sûrement contre les haines dont elles sont l'objet ou simplement par suite d'une sorte d'émulation, s'efforcent d'être supérieures en savoir aux populations qui les entourent' (*LS*: 169).

BIBLIOGRAPHY

Andersen, H., Bruun, H.H. and Kaspersen, L.B. (2003) 'Indledning', in H. Andersen, H.H. Bruun and L.B. Kaspersen (eds): *Max Weber: Udvalgte tekster*, vols I, II, Copenhagen: Hans Reitzel Publishers.

Andersson, S. (1977) *Som om. Skiss till ett porträt av Max Weber*, Gothenburg: Bokförlaget Korpen.

Aron, R. (1968) *Main Currents in Sociological Thought* (II), London: Weidenfeld & Nicolson.

Bendix, R. (1980) 'Two Sociological Traditions', in R. Bendix and G. Roth (eds): *Scholarship and Partisanship: Essays on Max Weber*, Berkeley, CA: University of California Press.

Bruun, H.H. (1972) *Science, Values and Politics in Max Weber's Methodology*, Copenhagen: Munksgaard.

Bruun, H.H. (2007) *Science, Values and Politics in Max Weber's Methodology (New Expanded Edition)*, Aldershot and Burlington, VT: Ashgate.

Cartwright, B.C. and Schwartz, R.D. (1973) 'The Invocation of Legal Norms: An Empirical Investigation of Durkheim and Weber', *American Sociological Review*, 3 (June): 340–54.

Coser, L. (1987) 'Preface', in Arthur Mitzman: *The Iron Cage: An Historical Interpretation of Max Weber*, New Brunswick, NJ and Oxford: Transaction.

Craib, I. (1997) *Classical Social Theory*, Oxford: Oxford University Press.

Durkheim, É. (1950 (1938)) *The Rules of Sociological Method*, trans. S.A. Solovay and J.H. Mueller, G.E.G. Catlin (ed.), Glencoe, IL: The Free Press.

Durkheim, É. (1978 (1893)) *De la division du travail social*, Paris: Quadrige/PUF.

Bibliography   119

Durkheim, É. (1981 (1895)) *Les règles de la méthode sociologique*, Paris: Quadrige/PUF.

Durkheim, É. (1981 (1897)) *Le suicide – étude de sociologie*, Paris: Quadrige/PUF.

Durkheim, E. (1994 (1984)) *The Division of Labour in Society*, trans. W.D. Halls, Houndmills, Basingstoke and London: The Macmillan Press.

Durkheim, É. (2010 (1952)) *Suicide. A Study in Sociology*, trans. J.A. Spaulding and G. Simpson, G. Simpson (ed.), London and New York: Routledge.

Eliaeson, E. (2002) *Max Weber's Methodologies*, Cambridge: Polity Press.

Eliaeson, S. (1988) 'Max Weber', in M. Bertilsson and B. Hansen (eds): *Samhällsvetenskapens klassiker*, Lund: Studentlitteratur.

Fivelsdal, E. (1972) 'Indledning', in É. Durkheim: *Den sociologiske metode*, Copenhagen: Fremad.

Fivelsdal, E. (1976) 'Fra klosteret til fabrikken', in M. Weber: *Den protestantiske etik og kapitalismens ånd*, Copenhagen: Fremad.

Gane, M. (2011) *On Durkheim's Rules of Sociological Method*, London and New York: Routledge.

Gephart, W. (2010) 'Einleitung', in Horst Baier *et al.* (eds): *Max Weber Gesamtausgabe (Max Weber: Wirtschaft und Gesellscahft, die Wirtschaft und die gesellschaftlichen Ordnungen und Mächte. Nachlass, Teilband 3, Recht, herausgegeben von Werner Gephart und Siegfried Hermes)*, vols 22–3, Tübingen: Verlag von J.C.B. Mohr (Paul Siebeck).

Giddens, A. (1981) *Capitalism and Modern Social Theory: An Analysis of the Writings of Marx, Durkheim and Max Weber*, Cambridge: Cambridge University Press.

Giddens, A. (1984a) *New Rules of Sociological Method: A Positive Critique of Interpretative Sociologies*, London: Hutchinson.

Giddens, A. (1984b) *The Constitution of Society: Outline of the Theory of Structuration*, Cambridge: Polity Press.

Giddens, A. (1986) *Durkheim*, London: Fontana Press.

Giddens, A. (1987) 'Weber and Durkheim: Coincidence and Divergence', in W. Mommsen and J. Osterhammel (eds): *Max Weber and his Contemporaries*, London: Allen & Unwin.

Gilbert, D. (1976) 'Social Values and Social Science: An Examination of the Methodological Writings of Weber and Durkheim', *Cornell Journal of Social Relations*, 11 (1): 23–9.

Gould, M. (1993) 'Legitimation and Justification: The Logic of Moral and Contractual Solidarity in Weber and Durkheim', in B. Agger (ed.): *Current Perspectives in Social Theory*, Greenwich/London: JAI Press.

Guneriussen, W. (2000) 'Emile Durkheim', in H. Andersen and L.B. Kaspersen (eds): *Klassisk og moderne samfundsteori*, Copenhagen: Hans Reitzel Publishers.

Hamilton, P. (1991) 'Editor's Foreword', in K. Thompson: *Emile Durkheim*, New York: Routledge.

120 Bibliography

Hillmann, J. (2002) 'Max Weber. The Protestant Ethic and the Spirit of Capitalism. New Translation and Introduction by Stephen Kalberg. Max Weber. The Protestant Ethic and the "Spirit" of Capitalism and Other Writings. Edited, Translated, and with an Introduction and Notes by Peter Baehr and Gordon C. Wells', *Canadian Journal of Sociology Online*, November–December 2002 (www.cjsonline.ca/pdf/pesc.pdf).

Hughes, J.A., Sharrock, W.W. and Martin, P.J. (2003) *Understanding Classical Sociology: Marx, Weber, Durkheim*, London: Sage Publications.

Jacobsen, B. (1991) *Max Weber og Friedrich Albert Lange. Max Webers rationalitets-sociologi: en anti-filosofi. Rødder tilbage til Friedrich Albert Lange?*, Aarhus: Department of Political Science, Aarhus University.

Kapsis, R.E. (1977) 'Weber, Durkheim, and the Comparative Method', *Journal of the History of the Behavioral Sciences*, 13: 354–68.

Lemert, C. (2005) 'Foreword – 1905: Weber in the Year of Miracles', in W.H. Swatos, Jr and L. Kalber (eds): *The Protestant Ethic Turns 100. Essays on the Century of the Weber Thesis*, Boulder, CO and London: Paradigm Publishers.

Lester, D. (ed.) (1994) *Emile Durkheim. Le Suicide. One Hundred Years Later*, Philadelphia, PA: The Charles Press, Publishers.

Lukes, S. (1988) *Émile Durkheim. His Life and Work: A Historical and Critical Study*, New York: Penguin Books.

Lundquist, A. (1983) 'Max Weber', in Max Weber: *Ekonomi och Samhälle. Förståendesociologins grunder*, Lund: Argos.

Månsson, P. (2000) 'Max Weber', in H. Andersen and L.B. Kaspersen (eds): *Klassisk og moderne samfundsteori*, Copenhagen: Hans Reitzel Publishers.

Marx, K. (1962 (1867)) *Das Kapital. Kritik der politischen Ökonomie* (Erster Band, Buch 1), vol. 23, Berlin: Dietz Verlag.

Mitzman, A. (1987) *The Iron Cage: An Historical Interpretation of Max Weber*, New Brunswick, NJ and Oxford: Transaction.

Mohseni, N. (1994) 'The Nature of Human and Social World for Marx, Weber, and Durkheim: A Hermeneutic Analysis', *Michigan Sociological Review*, 8: 84–94.

Morrison, K.L. (1990) 'Social Life and External Regularity: A Comparative Analysis of the Investigative Methods of Durkheim and Weber', *International Journal of Comparative Sociology*, XXXI (1–2): 93–103.

Müller, H.-P. (1992) 'Gesellschaftliche Moral und individuelle Lebensführung. Ein Vergleich von Emile Durkheim und Max Weber', *Zeitschrift für Soziologie*, 21 (1): 49–60.

Münch, R. (2004) 'Max Weber and Emile Durkheim in Dialogue: Classical Views on Contemporary Problems', in C. Camic and H. Joas (eds): *The Dialogical Turn: New Roles for Sociology in the Postdisciplinary Age*, New York and London: Rowman & Littlefield.

Bibliography   121

Nilsen, R.Å. (2003) *Metodologisk individualisme og kollektivisme hos Max Weber og Emile Durkheim*, Steinkjer: Højskolen i Nord-Trøndelag (Report no. 9).

Østerberg, D. (1988) 'Emile Durkheim', in M. Bertilsson and B. Hansen (eds): *Samhällsvetenskapens klassiker*, Lund: Studentlitteratur.

Parkin, F. (1991) *Max Weber*, New York and London: Routledge.

Parsons, T. (1964) *The Social System*, New York: The Free Press.

Parsons, T. (1968) *The Structure of Social Action: A Study of Social Action with Reference to a Group of Recent European Writers*, New York: The Free Press.

Ritzer, G. and Goodman, D.J. (2003) *Sociological Theory*, Boston: McGraw-Hill.

Roth, G. (1989) 'Marianne und ihr Kreis' (Einleitung), in M. Weber: *Max Weber. Ein Lebensbild*, München: R. Piper GmbH & Co. KG.

Schelting, A. von (1934) *Max Webers Wissenschaftslehre*, Tübingen: Verlag von J.C.B. Mohr (Paul Siebeck).

Schmid, M. (1994) 'Idealiserung und Idealtyp. Zur Logik der Typenbildung bei Max Weber', G. Wagner and H. Zipprian (eds): *Max Webers Wissenschaftslehre, Interpretation und Kritik*, Frankfurt a.M.: Suhrkamp.

Schroeter, G. (1986) 'Lettre à l'éditeur. Reading the Small Print, or the Weber/Durkheim Unawareness Puzzle Revisited', *Archives européennes de sociologie*, XXVII: 195–6.

Segre, S. (1986–7) 'On Max Weber's Awareness of Emile Durkheim', *History of Sociology: An International Review*, vols 6.2, 7.1 and 7.2 (combined issue): 151–67.

Seidmann, S. (1977) 'The Durkheim/Weber "Unawareness Puzzle"', *Archives européennes de sociologie*, XVIII: 356.

Sica, A. (2004) *Max Weber: A Comprehensive Bibliography*, New Brunswick, NJ and London: Transaction.

Sutherland, D.E. (1970) 'Conceptual Needles in Theoretical Haystacks: The Notion of Conflict in Durkheim and Weber', *Kansas Journal of Sociology*, VI (1): 37–56.

Szakolczai, A. (1996) *Durkheim, Weber and Parsons and the Founding Experiences of Sociology*, Firenze: European University Institute (EUI Working Paper SPS No. 96/11).

Taube, C.A. (1966) 'The Science of Sociology and Its Methodology: Durkheim and Weber Compared', *The Kansas Journal of Sociology*, 2 (4): 145–52.

Tenbruck, F.H. (1994) 'Die Wissenschaftslehre Max Webers. Voraussetzungen zu ihrem Verständnis', in G. Wagner and H. Zipprian (eds): *Max Webers Wissenschaftslehre. Interpretation und Kritik*, Frankfurt a.M.: Suhrkamp.

Theunissen, M. (1965) *Der Andere. Studien zur Sozialontologie der Gegenwart*, Berlin: Walter de Gruyter & Co.

Thompson, K. (1990) *Emile Durkheim*, New York and London: Routledge.

122 Bibliography

Tiryakian, E.A. (1966) 'A Problem for the Sociology of Knowledge: The Mutual Unawareness of Émile Durkheim and Max Weber', *Archives européennes de sociologie*, VII: 330–6.

Tiryakian, E.A. (1975) 'Neither Marx nor Durkheim . . . Perhaps Weber', *The American Journal of Sociology*, 81 (1): 1–33.

Turner, S.P. (1986) *The Search for a Methodology of Social Science: Durkheim, Weber, and the Nineteenth-Century Problem of Cause, Probability, and Action*, Dordrecht, Boston, MA, Lancaster and Tokyo: D. Reidel.

Wagner, G. and Zipprian, H. (1994) 'Max Webers Wissenschaftslehre – was ist das überhaupt? Zur Quellenlage und zum Stand der Rezeption', in G. Wagner and H. Zipprian (eds): *Max Webers Wissenschaftslehre. Interpretation und Kritik*, Frankfurt a.M.: Suhrkamp.

Weber, M. (1922) *Gesammelte Aufsätze zur Wissenschaftslehre*, Tübingen: Verlag von J.C.B. Mohr (Paul Siebeck).

Weber, M. (1981 (1904–5)) *Die protestantische Ethik I. Eine Aufsatzsammlung* (herausgegeben von J. Winckelmann), Gütersloh: Gütersloher Verlagshaus Mohn.

Weber, M. (1982) *Gesammelte Aufsätze zur Wissenschaftslehre* (fünfte erneut durchgesehene Auflage herausgegeben von J. Winckelmann), Tübingen: Verlag von J.C.B. Mohr (Paul Siebeck).

Weber, M. (1989) *Max Weber. Ein Lebensbild*, München: R. Piper GmbH & Co. KG.

Weber, M. (2009 (2004)) 'Basic Sociological Concepts', trans. K. Tribe, in S. Whimster (ed.): *The Essential Weber: A Reader*, London and New York: Routledge.

Weber, M. (2010 (1930)) *The Protestant Ethic and the Spirit of Capitalism*, trans. T. Parsons, introduction by A. Giddens, London and New York: Routledge.

Weber, M. (2011) *Collected Methodological Writings*, trans. H.H. Bruun and S. Whimster (eds), London and New York: Routledge.

Zeitlin, I.M. (2001) *Ideology and the Development of Sociological Theory*, Upper Saddle River, NJ: Prentice Hall.